TOP TIPS

FOR GIRLS

TOP TIPS

FOR GIRLS

KATE REARDON

headline

First published in 2008
by HEADLINE PUBLISHING GROUP

1

Cataloguing in Publication Data is available from the British Library

ISBN 978 0 7553 4314 0

Designed by Fiona Andreanelli

Typeset in Times and GillSans by Avon DataSet Ltd, Bidford on Avon, Warwickshire

Printed and bound in Great Britain by Clays Ltd, St Ives plc

Headline's policy is to use papers that are natural, renewable and recyclable products and made from wood grown in sustainable forests. The logging and manufacturing processes are expected to conform to the environmental regulations of the country of origin.

HEADLINE PUBLISHING GROUP
An Hachette Livre UK Company
338 Euston Road
London NW1 3BH

www.headline.co.uk

For my family

Contents

Introduction

When my brother and I were little and complained of a sore throat my mother would make us sleep wearing her infamous lard and nutmeg plaster around our necks. It was a piece of cotton (usually ripped from an old T-shirt) three to four inches wide, spread with lard and sprinkled with ground nutmeg. Yes, it was disgusting and we fought its application tooth and claw, but more annoyingly it actually worked. She still maintains that it's a Victorian remedy, passed to her from her mother and used as far back as her grandmother's own childhood in 1870.

This is what *Top Tips for Girls* is all about – not necessarily torture of small children with spices and animal fats, but simply about collecting all those little tips and tricks which we either work out for ourselves or which have been passed down the generations.

Due to pressure of work, parenthood or simple geography many women feel isolated, and so, when disaster big or small strikes, we have to reinvent the wheel and figure everything out for ourselves afresh. In the old days we inherited our grandmother's housewifery notes covering everything from furniture polish to beauty tips, complete with additions and corrections from our mothers and aunts. Nowadays, instead of turning to these family-written encyclopaedias, we seek guidance from chic and fabulous lifestyle gurus who can't remember the last time they did their own laundry.

So to create a compendium of real women's hard-won wisdom I started the website toptipsforgirls.com. Covering every conceivable aspect of modern life, the website is written by the women who visit it; none claim to be experts, but some may share the best way to stop a toddler's tantrum and others may have discovered the all-time greatest exfoliation method. *Top Tips for Girls* is about the sisterhood; it has been created by women all over the world from Honolulu to Beijing – women who may have little in common other than having access to a computer and knowing what it's like to battle unruly hair. They have all been generous enough to share what works for them and for that I thank them wholeheartedly.

A woman's tips can be a window into her personality. There are some from whom the question, How to get revenge? elicits the wholesome advice to live well and be happy. Others prefer taping raw fish under his car seat. When I was starting the website I asked my mother for any more top tips she had, specifically on the subject of parenthood. She replied with this corker, 'How to get your teenager to communicate: Talk to your teenagers while you're apparently absorbed in something else (cooking, ironing, sewing, driving etc). You'll get more information without eye contact.' I merrily typed it into the site and then it dawned on me – virtually every single important conversation I had had with my mother up to the age of about twenty-five was to the back of her head.

This book is a compilation of the best tips so far submitted to the website. They run from the straightforwardly practical, such as How to remove fake tan streaks, to the more poignant, such as How to cope with bereavement. Some may seem pretty weird, but worth a try – who knew that you could iron your clothes using hair straighteners? As in life, sometimes there are multiple solutions for one problem, such as: How to get over him and How to be happy.

As one wise tipster said, 'We're here for a good time, not for a long time.' So don't learn everything the hard way, listen to the women who have been there, done that and washed the stained T-shirt.

Here are my all-time favourite top ten tips. Some I owe to wonderful friends, my mother, grandmother or even great-grandmother, while others I worked out for myself by virtue of being on a date and having food stuck in my teeth.

How to get food out of your teeth when you're nowhere near a toothbrush

This is the SOLE benefit of being a smoker . . . you can use the cellophane from a packet of cigarettes as emergency dental floss.

How to pull clothes over your head without ruining your makeup

If you need to pull clothes over your head and you've already done your makeup, put a large old pair of knickers on your head so that they cover your face. They will protect your clothes and your makeup.

How to get to sleep AND be happy

I was recently taught the Horizontal Rule: when you are horizontal you are not allowed to think about anything that requires a solution. This is because, in the middle of the night, your left-side, problem-solving brain is fast asleep and your right-side, drama queen brain is wide awake. Instead, the only thing you are allowed to do is to count your blessings or think of five things you are grateful for that day. If you are still awake you have to think of five things you were grateful for yesterday, and the day before and the day before and so on. Not only does this actually get me to sleep, it makes me a happier, nicer person.

How to stop choking

If you're choking (and there is no obstruction that would require the Heimlich manoeuvre) the quickest way to regain your composure is to raise your arms above your head. It does something to your chest, lungs or diaphragm – whatever, it works.

How to know when you have too many clothes

I have a certain number of 'nice' hangers. When I start having to use those wire ones from the dry cleaners I know it's time for a closet clear-out.

How to make an emergency fluff remover

Wind Sellotape, sticky side out, around your hand a few times and you have an instant fluff/pet hair remover.

How to stop losing your jewellery

If you take your jewellery off to wash your hands in a public bathroom, put it in your mouth. You'll never forget it's there or leave a precious ring in a service-station toilet again.

How to prevent blisters

If you're wearing new shoes without tights, rub your feet with Vaseline. No rubbing = no blisters. You can also use natural lip salve if your shoes start rubbing during the day.

How to measure things to share

The golden rule of sharing between two children is: one cuts, the other chooses.

How to be a popular godparent

Send your godchildren postcards whenever you go away on holiday or business. When you're little it means a lot to get your own mail.

The tips in this book are the opinions of people who have contributed to the website; I haven't rigorously tested all of them, they simply sounded as if they made good sense. So if you make holes in your sweaters, turn your eyebrows green or your family disowns you because you followed any of the tips in this book, then it's not my fault. (And if you chose to smear yourself with lard and nutmeg, my mother would probably like to hear from you.)

Clothes

or

I'm a chic and fabulous woman. And then I wake up

How to decide if you should buy it

The best advice my grandmother gave to me was: 'Just because they make it in your size does not mean you should wear it.' When you're in the changing room, look hard at yourself in the mirror and say those words . . . you'll never buy a mistake again.

vancouvergirl

Only buy clothes that make you want to do a small dance in the changing room.

benjizoot

I ask myself the question – do I look better/nicer in the item than in what I was wearing when I went into the changing room. If it's a yes, then I'll probably buy it. If it's a relief to take it off and get back into my old clothes, then it's a no!

jeyacalder

How to straighten out a collar or edge of clothing without getting the iron out

Use hair straighteners! Not sure if it will damage some fabrics but on cotton tops and stuff this works well.

janine

How to fix a loose thread on a sweater

To put a loose thread (or a pulled line) on a fine knitted sweater/cardigan back into its place, get a needle and push the thread through to the other side (i.e. the inside) and paint it lightly with clear nail varnish. This stops it from coming back out again and is invisible from the outside.

ariel1004

How to stop a ladder in your tights

Liquid glue is a good solution if you don't have any transparent nail varnish with you. You put just a little on both edges and by the inside part, then let the glue/varnish dry and that ladder will not go anywhere.

Xandri

How to unstick a zipper

If your zipper sticks, then rub a lead pencil on either side and it should run smoothly again.

MillieFox

Use a plain white bar of soap. Rub it on the zipper and it will wax it, making it run smoothly.

femme

How to repair or stop a zipper from splitting

I do a lot of dressmaking and find that the only safe way is to replace the zip. However, if it is a lightweight zip and has come apart near the base, you can try stitching over the teeth, as tightly as possible, with stitches very close together to hold it in place.

Finlandia

If the zip has started to part at the bottom, pin a safety-pin across it from the inside, just above the split. Only a tiny bar of metal will show on the outside and it will take the strain, thus stopping the zip from opening further, and also stopping the slider running off the bottom of the zip when you open it.

SallySproggs

How to make an emergency fluff remover

Put on rubber gloves and 'stroke' garment. Hairs and fluff removed.

sooz

How to fix a hem in an emergency

If the hem of your skirt or trousers comes undone, pretty much every office and restaurant in the world has a stapler you can borrow in an emergency. If you're wearing tights make sure the prongy bits face outwards.

Trula

How to avoid four butt cheeks

Wear proper sized, proper-fitted knickers. There's no point wearing a micro string thong if you have a lovely sexy curvy but macro-sized ass.

Slothie

How to always look pulled together

Always wear lipstick! The long-lasting ones with glossy topcoat come in neutral colours, and they don't come off every time you take a drink or kiss someone. My mum always told me that I shouldn't leave the house without lipstick, because I look dead without it . . . it took me too long to realise that she was right!

FrancesHouseman

Take a few minutes before bed to set out your outfit and accessories for the next day. Rushing is the easiest way to ruin your look!

CassandraM

How to sort and put away socks while having FUN

If you have a family and kids you can throw all the clean socks in a pile and have a game of 'matching' and the one with the most pairs wins. It's like the game where you turn over cards and find the matching animals or whatever . . . Every week the socks that don't have mates will be left, sparking a hunt or raising awareness of the socks that are missing in action. Maybe they will be found somewhere hiding!

babycakes

How to really clear out your wardrobe

Get someone else to help. My sister and/or daughter are great – they have no emotional tie with my clothes and have no hesitation if things are past their sell-by date or look awful (I'm sure you get the picture). I have space in my small wardrobe and the charity shop benefits.

Lynda

Don't forget to get rid of things that are just plain worn out. It's hard to get rid of something you've worn so much, but I always try to look at the thing objectively and I ask myself, 'If I saw this at the charity shop for £3, would I buy it?' If the answer is no, it should go in the rubbish.

EmilyD

I cleared out my wardrobe when I was really angry – which made me ruthless.

ahlh

How to achieve the perfect wardrobe

Organise your wardrobe to reflect your lifestyle – like a pie chart. If the majority of your life is spent at work, then the majority of your clothes should be work clothes. Your weekend and evening clothes should then take the minority of the space – and your spangles should take hardly any room at all! If you have more going-out clothes than work clothes and you only go out once a year – you're going to look great at work!

carriehelen

Accessories

or

Men have team sports, we have handbags

How to accessorise

A great tip about accessorising is to get dressed as normal, and then (if you're worried that you've over-accessorised) turn your back to the mirror. Turn around quickly and take off the first thing you see.

Justine

I work in fashion and have learnt that the key to accessorising is not to overdo it. Pick one great accessory, such as a statement belt or a work-of-art necklace, and focus your outfit on that point. Never wear dangly earrings with a necklace, and keep rings to a minimum.

Blondie

How to polish handbags

Clear furniture polish is the best polish for handbags.

AnyaHindmarch

How to be organised if you use several handbags

I use several favourite handbags and it is a hassle to keep putting the bare necessities into each one (lip gloss, tweezers, breath freshener, plasters etc). So I keep these in a clear plastic cosmetic bag that fits into all of my favourite handbags. When I change bags, I just grab the clear bag and pop it in the handbag that I will be using that day.

terryleecox

I have a few designer bags that I use at the weekend. I have them stocked with some of the essentials – hairbrush, lip gloss, a stash of mad money – so all I have to do is throw in my wallet and mobile phone. I found that it is really helpful to have a few extra sets of keys, so I can keep them in the extra bags as well.

Masi

How to remove water marks from a leather handbag

(I had a similar problem with my leather couch.) A friend told me to use baby wipes that have aloe in to clean it up and it worked like a charm! Using a soft, damp cloth with a couple of drops of baby oil will also do the trick.

maryzeee

How to check if pearls are real or not

Gently rub/tap the pearl against your teeth. If it feels very smooth it's fake. Real pearls feel slightly gritty.

waxy1086

How to look after real pearls

Apply your perfume, hairspray, creams and makeup etc before putting your pearls on. The harsh chemicals can damage the lustre. The nacre can become dull or marked. Don't put perfume on your neck if you are wearing pearls. Store them in a soft silk, satin or velvet pouch; never store them next to metals that can scratch the pearls. Pearls do love natural body oils, so wear then regularly. Clean them with a soft damp cloth after a few wears.

waxy1086

How to store jewellery

If your jewellery is in a mess and all you can see is a big pile of it, you'll never wear any of it. So store small pieces such as earrings and rings in ice cube trays. These stack easily too.

Judith

Save the tiny Ziploc bags that come on new clothing (with the extra button or thread) and drop your necklaces or earrings into these before stashing in your travel bag.

Sundance

How to clean diamonds

The best thing to use is washing up liquid and an old soft toothbrush. Remember to clean them in a bowl so there's no chance they can be washed down the sink!

mmaccaw

How to clean vintage costume jewellery

Please don't ever put rhinestones (vintage or otherwise) into water or chemical dips. Moisture will damage the foil backing, dulling the stones, and also can cause any type of glued-in stone to loosen. It's far safer to put a tiny bit of glass cleaner or sudsy water on a soft cloth and gently wipe the jewellery (if simply dusting doesn't work). Then dry it very quickly with a hairdryer set on cool. After collecting vintage and antique jewellery for twenty-five years and being a dealer for about ten years, I've learned it's always best to treat these jewels by the most conservative method possible. If in doubt, or faced with a really dirty piece, ask a jeweller to clean it safely for you.

glitzqueen

How to stop metal jewellery turning your skin green.

Paint it with clear nail varnish; it works on rings, bracelets and earrings. It also works on other items. I bought an expensive watch which had a chain-effect strap and it caused itchy red bumps, so I painted all the parts that touched my skin and now I can wear it with no problem.

livliv

How to wear a ring that's too big

You can buy ring grips from home-wares catalogues (you know, those grannified catalogues dropped through your letterbox) that are clear plastic/rubber split cylinders that you push on to the back of the ring. Alternatively, and bargainously, wrap cotton thread round the back till the desired size is achieved.

pearlgirl

How to get a stuck ring off your finger

Start by running your hand under very cold water. If that doesn't work, then wind sewing cotton tightly and evenly around your finger between the ring and the fingernail – starting at the nail end. Pass the end of the cotton under the ring and pull gently – this will unwind the string and ease the ring off.

Bianca

Apply washing up liquid to your finger to lubricate; the ring should come off quickly.

ysmith77

How to stop losing your jewellery

Thread rings on to your watch strap, fasten the catch and stick the lot down your bra. If you forget, the weird lump will surely attract comment.

psbarth47

Shoes
or
Did somebody say 'Sale'?

How to buy shoes

Always buy shoes after drinking one glass of wine (no more). Then you are a little adventurous but haven't lost the plot. Come to think of it, you should do nearly everything after just one glass of wine.

lolabelle

Buy shoes at the end of the day when your feet are at their most swollen.

Scarlett

How to buy high heels

Shift your weight around, try a little jump step, stand on one foot for a few seconds; if you can't do that then the heels are too high. After walking around for a few minutes, try walking backwards for three steps; if you can do that naturally, without feeling as if you're off balance, then you've found a good pair.

Masi

How to walk in high heels

Two words: Weight Back. I have literally stopped people who looked as though they couldn't walk in their heels, told them, and seen them have an 'ah ha!' moment.

Peachy503

Walk by putting one foot directly in front of the other. It makes such a difference and makes you feel sexier when you walk!

00jess00

How to avoid blisters while camping, hiking or backpacking

First put on a cheapo pair of pop socks (knee-high stockings) and then put on your socks and boots. Instead of your socks rubbing against your skin and creating blisters, the friction ends up between the hose and your socks instead. Voilà, no more blisters! Learned this in a backpacking club in school – a club where we regularly walked fifteen miles or so per day. This really works!

CeeVee

How to stop shoes rubbing

You can rub a dry cake of soap around the offending edge that is rubbing. This will make a nice waxy coating to stop the rubbing and allow you to wear the shoes long enough to soften the leather.

Ferny

How to deodorise shoes

Put the shoes in a plastic bag and then in the freezer overnight. This kills the bacteria that cause the odour.

patsharp

You can deodorise smelly trainers and walking shoes by sprinkling them with baking soda.

Chantal

How to clean flip-flops

I hate it when the inside soles of my flip-flops get dirty, so I clean them with wet wipes. It works a treat.

Luz

This sounds disgusting but you can put all-rubber flip-flops into the dishwasher on a cool programme!

Judi

How to disguise scuffed heels

Especially if they are a dark colour and the plastic heel has been exposed, you can try colouring in the scuff with a black marker pen. I do it to all my shoes, even the Jimmy Choos!

Odette

How to store boots

Take an old magazine and roll it. Stick the roll inside the leg of the boot – it will keep the top portion of the boot from flopping over in your closet and the ankle portion won't wrinkle or wear away as quickly. Note though – make sure the magazine you put in one boot is the same size as the one you put in the other.

paulinast

How to squeeze on tight boots

If you are trying to put on boots and your legs are too clammy or the boots have a rough interior that prevents them sliding nicely up your leg, put your foot into the point of a plastic carrier bag and pull the boot on over the bag. Once the boot is up smoothly, pull the plastic bag until it breaks, and pull it up and out of the boot.

Penelope

How to get rid of marks on light-coloured shoes

Rub with a little toothpaste on a clean dry cloth. The marks will soon disappear. Toothpaste is also good for getting marks off leather furniture.

jontrv2

How to clean patent leather

I used to clean my patent shoes and bags with whatever came to hand but to give a lovely shine, put a wee smear of Vaseline on a soft cloth and buff in.

thepoet

How to stretch shoes

To soften shoe leather: cut a potato up and stuff it into the area that you want stretched or softened. Leave the potato overnight. It works – don't ask me how but it does.

Barbaric

Use a hairdryer on them for about twenty to thirty seconds until they are thoroughly warmed up, then put them on and they should stretch and mould to your feet.

triciab1023

Cooking

or

Serving food at a different temperature from when you
bought it doesn't count

How to slice an onion without crying

This sounds really bizarre I know – but suck on a teaspoon while
chopping. It does work.

pearlgirl

Light a candle near where you are chopping – it burns off the fumes
which make you cry.

vernbug

How to stop a pan from boiling over

When you are making pasta or rice, place a wooden spoon across the pan
and the bubbles will not rise above it.

LevantineLass

How to crush an Oxo cube and keep your fingers clean

Before removing the foil, crush the cube inside and then tear off the
corner and tip the contents out – so simple and it saves the stock cube
powder sticking to your fingers!

spagirl

How to cut a pizza

No pizza cutter? Use a pair of scissors instead.

Ursie

How to make perfect biscuits or piecrust

Use frozen, grated butter or shortening instead of butter or shortening that's only been chilled.

CeeVee

How to keep cling film from snarling

Keep cling film in the freezer. It seems to give the wrap just enough body and structure to allow it to be rolled off, sheared, and placed over your food without curling up or snarling.

Abellamiento

How to remove a burned-on black stain from a saucepan

If your saucepan boils dry, soak overnight with a dishwasher tablet to remove the black burn stain.

LadyHelenTaylor

Fill it with cola and leave overnight – wash it in the morning and the burned bits will all come off.

janhumphries

How to stop avocado going brown in a salad

Put the stone into the salad bowl until ready to serve, this will keep the avocado green.

LittleBear

How to ripen avocados

Put them in a fruit bowl with ripe bananas.

beautybunnikin

How to stop a chopping board sliding around

Putting a wet piece of kitchen towel under a chopping board stops the board from sliding around your kitchen worktop.

pgrier

How to buy fish

Make sure the eyes are still clear. Cloudy eyes = out of the water a few days.

pippinpuss

How to always have lemon wedges handy

To store a ready supply of lemon wedges for drinks, fish and cooking, slice and de-pip lemon slices, roll one by one into a long strip of cling film and freeze. Individual slices don't stick to each other, defrost in minutes and are even better in drinks than flabby fresh ones.

Violet

How to not waste a whole lemon

Rather than wasting a whole lemon if you just need a little juice, make a small hole in it and squeeze out what you need.

Zenobia

How to get more juice out of a lemon

If you gently heat lemons before squeezing them you get a lot more juice.

Kimberley

How to get unwaxed lemons

If you can only get hold of waxed lemons you can de-wax them by briefly 'dunking' them into a pan of boiling water, dry thoroughly, et voilà!

Joolz

How to make great roast potatoes

After you've par-boiled them, add a little flour, hold the lid firmly on the pan and shake them vigorously to give super fluffy edges – they'll go doubly crispy.

Margot

How to serve roast potatoes FAST

You can roast potatoes in advance and freeze them. To serve, put them into a hot oven for fifteen minutes.

Portia

How to cook baked potatoes faster

If you put a metal skewer through the middle and leave it there while cooking, it will act as a heat conductor and the potato will cook faster.

Sharon

How to make good gravy

Put ice cubes into your roasting tin after removing your roasted meat. This solidifies the fat after a few minutes, which can be removed in a nice block. Then simply add in your stock, and/or flavouring e.g. Marmite! You then have an excellent lower fat gravy.

prowsec

How to make a roast super-tender

Cook a joint between two roasting pans of the same size. Take off the top one for the last fifteen minutes. The meat will be very tender as it's been steamed as well as roasted.

Helga

How to keep the fridge smelling sweet

Keep a little open pot of bicarbonate of soda in the back of the fridge.

Myrtle

How to get all the honey or other sticky stuff out of a measuring cup

Normally sticky stuff coats the measuring cup, so you end up with less than you thought in the bowl. So very, very lightly oil the measuring cup before you pour in the honey.

Zenobia

Dip the measuring cup or spoon in boiling water before you put it into the sticky stuff, which will slide off easily.

joesaunt

How to unbrown onions or garlic

When browning onions/garlic and they get a bit more toasted than you'd like, simply add a tablespoon of water to your pan and the brown edges disappear.

Alessandra

How to stop milk burning

Put a large marble in the pan. The marble automatically stirs the milk and prevents it from burning.

Tracy

How to test if an egg has gone off

Fill a pan with water. Bad eggs will float to the top, good ones lie flat on the bottom.

Chelsea

Hold the egg to your ear and shake it. If the egg is fresh, you should not be able to hear the contents slurping around at all.

scifidiva

How to stop eggs from cracking when boiled

Pierce a tiny hole in one end of the egg with a very sharp knife or pin before you put it in the water. That will allow any air to escape as it expands, rather than cracking your egg.

Kaitlyn

How to make the perfect poached egg

Before cracking your eggs into a pan of simmering water, gently place each egg (uncracked) into the water for about twenty seconds. Take these out of the water, stir the water to create a whirlpool then crack the eggs into it. Placing the eggs uncracked in the water first binds the egg white together, so that you have a nice rounded poached egg, instead of egg white spreading throughout the whole pan (which it does the older the egg).

jojo28

How to beat eggs

Adding a little water to the eggs you are beating makes them lighter and less hard work.

Regina

How to get all the baked beans out of the tin

By storing your baked bean tins upside down, when it comes to opening them (right way up) all the beans will slide out easily as the sauce will have collected at the bottom of the tin

Annie

How to tenderise meat

Rub it with kiwi fruit.

Holly

How not to shred your fingers on a cheese grater

Wear a rubber glove. It will be grated before your fingers!

patsharp

How to use up the end of a bottle of wine

Simply pour red wine into an ice cube tray, freeze and save, for tasty flavour in casseroles and stews – try it!

yvonne1987

How to avoid a fire caused by frying in hot oil

If your oil is getting too hot, turn down the stove and add more oil, as the cold oil will immediately bring the temperature down. Emergency averted.

beagirl2

How to prevent soggy tomato sandwiches

For a BLT put the tomato in the middle with bacon on the bottom and lettuce on top. Works every time.

BRILYN

How to cut open a passion fruit

Don't cut the fruit in half, cut it near the top, as you would a soft-boiled egg. That way you can scoop out the passion fruit pulp with a teaspoon rather than lose most of it on to the cutting board.

dimlay

How to open a soda bottle without it fizzing over

Twist the cap gently. After you hear the first fizz, stop and wait for the fizz to calm down. It should be safe to open now, but if it continues to fizz up keep stopping and waiting. I learned this after a particularly embarrassing episode in the St James's Mall, Edinburgh when my Irn Bru bottle exploded and I had to get down on my hands and knees to clean it up, to the applause of the watching public.

sproglet

How to dry out lettuce

If you want to dry the lettuce after washing it and before using it, put it into the middle of a tea towel, join all four corners together and hold on to them. Go outdoors and spin the tea towel around over your head, or with your arm doing big circles. This removes lots of excess water from the lettuce and the kids love watching you in case you let go of one of the corners!

COLIYTYHE

How to keep lettuce fresh

Add a paper towel to the bag. It will absorb the moisture and keep the lettuce from going slimy too soon.

Frida

How to make a limp lettuce crisp again

Put the lettuce leaves into a bowl of cold water with a piece of coal. After about ten minutes the lettuce will become as crisp as a fresh one. It works well with limp cabbage leaves as well.

maudessa

How to prepare a cake tin

Whether or not the recipe tells you to, grease AND flour the cake tin. Makes removing the cake a zillion times easier. For a chocolate cake, don't use flour in the tin . . . instead, 'flour' the greased tin with unsweetened cocoa. Works perfectly, and you won't have weird white streaks on the cake when you turn it out!

CeeVee

How to portion a cream cake without squelching

When filling a cake with cream, cut the top layer into portions and reassemble on top of the filling.

clinic2316

How to get onion or garlic smell off your hands

With dish soap in your hands, rub them against anything stainless steel (e.g. a spoon or the tap) under cool/lukewarm water. Fancy kitchen stores sell stainless steel 'bars' that look like traditional soap for this purpose; however, there is really no need to invest in that when a regular old spoon does the trick.

DezG

How to make perfect whipped cream

Grab a bag of frozen peas or sweetcorn and place it beneath the bowl.
The cold makes the cream whip faster – no muss no fuss.

fashionvictim

How to extend the life of a banana

Contrary to popular opinion, bananas can be kept in the fridge once they
have become yellow and ripe. Although the skin will become black, the
fruit itself will remain the same for up to a week. Have done this for
years.

AudreyT800

How to stop salt from clogging up the salt shaker

Put a few grains of uncooked rice in with the salt. They will absorb
moisture, but are too big to come out of the holes.

Natalie

How to fake homemade mayonnaise

To impress your guests with homemade-tasting mayonnaise, add fresh
lemon (or lime) juice and capers or thyme to ordinary mayo – makes a
tasty spread for sandwiches, grilled fish or poached chicken.

Deborah

How to peel apples and tomatoes easily

If you pour scalding water over apples or tomatoes before peeling them,
the skin will just slip off.

Tamsen

How to crush things without making a mess

To crush crackers or biscuits quickly and neatly, place in a plastic bag,
then roll with a rolling pin.

Eileen

How to clear honey that's gone cloudy

If your runny honey is looking a bit murky, stick it, without the lid, in the microwave for a bit and it will clear.

Kendra

How to cook delicious carrots for a roast

Put the carrots into a saucepan with NO WATER AT ALL. Put a large dollop of butter on the top (a quarter of one of those standard UK butter blocks) and two dessertspoons of sugar. Cover the saucepan with a lid, and put it on the lowest heat possible for about thirty minutes, checking it occasionally to make sure nothing's burnt. The carrots will poach in the butter and their own liquid, and start to caramelise in the sugar. Not one for the health freaks, admittedly, but given that everything enjoyable is either illegal, immoral or fattening, here's to enjoyment!

pgrier

How to find the best cookery book for REAL beginners

Visit your library and borrow a child's first cookbook or something like that. They have simple instructions and great pictures. Have fun and (as I tell my household) eat with your mouth (taste) not with your eyes!

COLIYTYHE

Gardening

How to aerate your lawn

Forget fancy machines or backbreaking work, just wander up and down wearing your golf spikes.

Polly

How to sow tiny seeds

Sow tiny seeds from a spice shaker.

Candace

How to keep your fingernails clean while gardening

Before you start, dig your nails into a bar of soap – it really works! Better than gloves for me, because even if I wear gloves I always take them off to do something finicky. Thus, I do the soap thing then put on gloves.

DezG

How to discourage weeds and grass from growing on your patio

Every so often pour a bucket of very hot, very very salty water over your patio.

Ilana

How to get out of turning your compost every few weeks

Add a handful of worms; they will aerate it for you.

Cindy

How to make compost of leaves and grass cuttings

You can make useful compost in one season out of a mixture of leaves and grass cuttings, but not of either one alone.

Joan

How to take care of your eyes when gardening

When pruning, always cut the branches nearest you first. If you reach past them your eyes will focus on the back branches and you risk being jabbed, possibly seriously.

Cali

How to weed amongst delicate plants

The best weeding tool is a curved grapefruit knife. With its serrated edge, pointed end and curved blade you can extract weeds without hurting delicate plants.

Cali

How to deter slugs

Scatter bark mulch around the base of plants, especially hostas, to deter slugs. Apparently prickly surfaces hurt their little 'paws'.

Peggy

Put a bowl of beer at the bottom of the afflicted plant or tree. Slugs and snails love it and will drown in it. Expect to find a full bowl in the morning. Cruel? But very effective.

Mimi

This works on your garden pot plants. Just spray around the top of the pot with WD 40 every couple of weeks. The slugs hate it!

patsharp

How to kill greenfly organically

Soak rhubarb leaves in a bucket of water for a few weeks and use the resulting liquid on your plants. Warning – it does really smell!

Gwiddon

How to deter cats from fouling in your garden

I find that mothballs sprinkled around the garden deter the felines.

Redlady

Sprinkle ground cayenne pepper on the soil every two to three months.

maryzeee

Squirt the little intruders with a water pistol; cats hate getting wet and won't come back if you aim at them a couple of times. It may sound cruel but it has worked in my garden.

Anita123

How to get rid of dandelions from your lawn

Place a pinch of salt in the centre of the rosette of leaves. The plant will die, but be careful not to get salt on the grass or any other plants as it will kill them too.

LadyB

How to make flowering branches last in the vase

Cut flowering branches at an angle, and then hammer the heck out of the bottom four to six inches (I do this outside, in our driveway, using a rock and pounding the bottom portion of the branch directly against the tarmac – no clean-up necessary, so it's far easier than if you try to do it inside the house). This splays out the wood so that the branch can suck up water more efficiently. If you don't do this, they won't even look good in the vase for a full day. If you try this, you'll see that they look good for three to five days.

CeeVee

How to design raised vegetable beds

When constructing raised beds for vegetables, set them at comfortable working height (not knee height), and no wider than you can reach to the middle from either side.

Zsazsa

How to perk up ferns

You can perk up wilted potted ferns by watering them once a month with very weak tea.

Valerie

One can also use banana peel – just place banana skins around the ferns. There is a lot of goodness in banana skins for plants.

Spatchy

How to keep houseplants shiny

Polish their leaves with banana skins.

Mya

How to protect your plants, fruit and vegetables from pests

Plant marigolds nearby – they seem to deter lots of pests.

Eve

How to stop mosquitoes breeding in your water barrel

Pour in a tiny bit of cooking oil.

Iola

How to use the soot from your fireplace

It is great for drying out an over-wet compost bin, and also helps the composting process. I also use the ashes from a bonfire.

kimberly l

How to give your seedlings the best start

Save the cardboard inners of toilet rolls for sewing seeds in, so that early roots grow long and strong.

Felicia

How to sort good seeds from bad ones

Pour the seeds into a shallow bucket of water. By morning the good seeds will have sunk and the bad ones will be floating on top. Be sure to plant the good seeds immediately.

Crystal

How to stop garden tools from rusting

Keep them in a bucket of sand.

Magda

How to water your garden pots more easily

Before filling the pot, take an empty plastic bottle and make small holes all over it, then cut the top off to make a wider neck. Place the bottle in the middle of one of your larger flower pots in the garden and cover with earth with the neck still exposed. You can now fill up the bottle with water; the small perforations will allow water to seep into the earth and keep it wet without making a mess. Just keep refilling the bottle with water when the earth is drying out.

WATERSIDE

Home

or
Martha Stewart, eat your heart out

How to make flowers stand upright in a vase

If you crisscross the top of your vase with Sellotape, making even sections one way, then the other way, it creates lots of squares. Place the stems in all the holes and the tape stops them falling over. You can put two or three in each hole depending on your spacing. Makes the flower arrangement look very professional.

WATERSIDE

Try putting some cling film/wrap over the top of the vase and poke the flowers through.

COLIYTYHE

How to keep cut flowers fresh

Put a dash of bleach into the water in flower vases. It keeps it clear and slime free and means you never have to refresh it.

Carmen

To keep roses and tulips upright, pierce a pin through the stem approximately one inch down from the flower. When the flower is cut it can cause an 'air lock' in the stem and when the 'air lock' reaches the bloom it stops food getting to the flower head.

Elaine

Trim the stems of the roses then plunge the ends into boiling water, counting up to thirty or until you can't see any more air bubbles coming from them. I've kept roses for up to three weeks using this method.

aswas

How to get rid of house flies

Put some eucalyptus oil on a cloth, open the door wide, and then wave the cloth vigorously, working towards the door. Flies will rapidly disappear.

Caroline

How to get rid of ants

Ants pretty much steer clear of anything that is 'powdery' so to speak. I believe it has to do with the fact that any powder disrupts their senses and makes their little legs not able to, say, climb a wall; they just fall right off. I've had really good luck with using baby powder.

lisaveronica

When I was young we always used baking soda. My mum read they would lick it off their feet so they could walk/climb and that it would expand in their tummies and that they would explode – kind of gruesome, but it has always been effective. It seems to be something we have around for cleaning, cooking, and deodorising anyway.

ramee151

How to clean work surfaces, windows and shiny metal without chemicals

For floors and counters use one part vinegar and three parts water. For glass use one part vodka, one part grapefruit juice and six parts water.

Amy

How to clean windows

Add dishwasher rinse aid to your bucket of water instead of soap etc.
This really works.

Moodykat

How to remove sticky labels

Use a hairdryer to remove labels that are stubbornly stuck on bottles,
bowls, even the soles of your shoes. Heat the label for a few seconds to
release the adhesive, then peel them off.

coulsonn

If you haven't got a hairdryer then use any oil-based product. Saturate
the label and then peel it off. Works like a charm!

DorBella

How to remove Sellotape sticky from glass

Get some nail polish remover on a bit of cotton wool and rub away!

buckridge

How to make a candle fit a too-small candlestick

To make a candle fit a candlestick, hold the end in very hot water and it
will soften enough to be jammed in tight.

Tawny

How to keep candles burning longer

Store them in the freezer – this will add hours of additional burn time.

Estelle

How to build a great log fire

If you want big flames build a tepee shape with the logs against the back
of the fireplace.

Belinda

How to stop a fire smoking up a room

To stop a room getting all smoky from an open fire, roll up a few sheets of newspaper, light them and hold them up the chimney before you light the fire. This will heat the chimney and create a draught that will suck the smoke upwards.

Melanie

How to survive a fire

The most important thing, especially if you have children, is to have a fire drill and practise it. That way everyone is less likely to panic. Try to figure out as many ways as possible out of each room and pre-arrange a specific meeting place outside the house.

Tracy

How to restore the flattened carpet underneath your furniture

Place a damp towel over the area and iron it. The steam will restore the carpet's natural fluff.

Chelsea

Leave a small ice cube in the indent. Once it melts and dries a bit, vacuum with the brush attachment.

JCF

How to clean lampshades

I keep a soft-bristled paintbrush around for this sort of task. It helps remove dust in tight ridges and grooves. I also use it for dusting bookcases and electronic equipment. Inexpensive and can be rinsed out.

melaniezelanie

How to list your possessions for insurance

It's much easier to go around the house videoing everything you own (with your own running commentary for details) than to write a huge list of all your possessions for insurance purposes. Just keep the video at work, so that if everything does go up in smoke, then the video won't go too.

Olga

How to keep keys and money safe

Get an empty mayonnaise jar, paint it cream inside and store all your keys and money in there. No burglar would ever suspect it!

wnknt

How to deter burglars

If you have a driveway and you are away in your car on holiday, ask neighbours if they would park one of their cars on your driveway while you are not there.

COLIYTYHE

Never leave your handbag or keys within easy reach of the front door. Keys can be 'fished' through the letterbox and used to gain entry.

Rhiannon

How to scare off intruders

If you're scared that there might be someone inside your house when you arrive home, ring your own doorbell and leave plenty of time before you let yourself in. It should scare them off.

Enola

How to get in if you get locked out

I did this when I had locked myself out. Take a wire out of your bra and insert it in the gap between the lock and door frame, then push until you lever the door open. This only works on old Chubb locks on wooden doors!

JETROX

How to change a duvet cover easily

Before attempting to put on a duvet cover, first turn it inside out. Then put a hand into each far corner inside. With hands still in the corners inside the cover, take a corner each side of one end of the duvet so that now you are holding the corners of the duvet and the inside-out corners of the cover together. Shake the duvet cover on to the duvet so that it drops over it and the right side is now in place.

eng

Following the above method, if you can drop both duvet and cover, holding the corners, over a stairwell and shake, even better. Try storing duvet sets inside one of the pillow cases: it saves a lot of time searching for a matching set when changing the bed.

josie

How to downsize to a smaller kitchen

A great tip for downsizing to a smaller kitchen is: instead of putting all utensils, cutlery, plates and glasses away in their usual place, put them in a separate box or tub each time you finish using them. Within a few weeks you will see exactly what you actually use, rather than all that junk that's just filling up your kitchen.

Helen

How to have a tidy house with no effort

Instead of sitting gazing moronically at dumb ads on TV, get up and do something useful during every commercial break. Tidying, cleaning a sink, sorting laundry, sorting paperwork, washing up etc all get done in short bursts without becoming a major task.

aitch

Each day, set an egg timer for fifteen minutes and get as MUCH done as you can in that time. Sadly, I get extra excited when I finish and realise I've done more than the day before. Ahh, the satisfaction.

CassandraM

How to get grease and fingerprints off the walls

Use a slice of white bread to rub off any dirt or stains. Try it, it really works!

yvonne1987

How to stop children's junk taking over the whole house

Let each child choose his or her own big box (mine chose a large, brightly coloured plastic one) and a smaller one. At the end of the day, we had 'tidy up time' and a treat for the tidiest (mine chose extra time in the bath or extra bubbles . . . they're teenagers now so those treats seem very tame!!). All the toys go into the big box. The smaller box holds crayons or 'losable' things, and is then put in the big box too. Therefore there is only one box to remove to the bedroom (or to hide behind the settee if mother-in-law is on the horizon!).

faylin4

How to make almost any abhorrent task go faster

Set a timer for thirty minutes and do nothing but that task while the timer is on. When the timer goes off, give yourself permission to be done! You've been productive and now you can take a break. I find this makes a big difference and helps me get done those tasks I don't particularly enjoy (but still have to do anyway!).

CeeVee

How to put away laundry

Always put fresh laundry UNDER the pile of similar things, or at the further reaches of your wardrobe. That way you'll actually wear all your T-shirts and pants, instead of the same three over and over again.

Tawny

How to get rid of a mildew smell in a washing machine

I had this problem for a while, but solved it permanently by putting neat bleach in the little drawer you normally put your powder in and running the washer on the hottest cycle possible. No more smell since and this was months ago. I did try it on a lower temperature, but the smell came back after a few weeks, but the ultra-hot wash plus the bleach did the trick.

AlleyKat

How to stop static from the dryer

Pour a bit of laundry softener on to an old facecloth and put it in with your drying.

Brianne

How to fluff up stiff towels

You can make old towels all soft and fluffy again by soaking them in washing soda. Then wash normally.

Fawn

How to hang sweaters on a washing line

Take an old pair of tights and thread the legs through the arms of your sweater so that the waist is sticking out through the neck. Then you can clip the feet and waistband of the tights to the line – it stops those annoying clippy marks.

Margot

How to get chewing gum out of fabrics

If the gum is embedded, rub with vinegar (preferably white) and the gum will break up and fall away.

Caprice

How to remove water marks on dark wood

A really yucky solution but it does work. If you have white water marks on mahogany or dark polished wood, mix a paste of olive oil and cigarette ash and work into the mark. It will come out, and the smell will disappear quite quickly!

Sage

It sounds pretty daunting, but metal polish does work. Put a little bit on a soft cloth and work it in over the water mark and then polish off with another clean soft cloth.

loops

How to protect walls from being marked by the top of a ladder

Tie old socks over the top ends of the ladder so that they don't mark the walls they're leant against.

Georgia

How to hang wallpaper

Hanging wallpaper is easier if you put the paste on the wall rather than the paper.

Scout

How to fill tiny cracks when painting woodwork

Add a bit of flour to your paint.

Fern

How to eliminate paint smells when decorating

Before painting, add a few drops of vanilla extract to the paint and mix it in well. If you're using white paint, make sure you get clear vanilla extract.

Inmop

How to remove paint from skin

For a non-irritating remover, use cooking oil.

Lara

How to make a room smell nice

Place a dryer sheet used in tumble dryers on the top of a radiator. When the radiator is on, the sheet warms up and the smell fills the room.

BarbaraClark

How to clean decanters and odd-shaped vases

To clean decanters fill a quarter of the way up with warm water, add crushed eggshell and shake about a bit.

Scout

Denture cleaner tabs are also effective, as is a small amount of washing powder or dishwasher powder. Just make sure the decanter is well washed afterwards – we don't drink whisky so didn't know that the expensive whisky in our newly cleaned decanter tasted soapy!

charpur

How to clean antique ivory piano keys

I heard that toothpaste is good on the white keys. It makes sense, because tusks are elephants' teeth after all.

ValW

How to remove scuff marks off lino flooring

Use WD 40 to remove marks left by shoes and trainers.

jackandclaire

How to keep silver clean easily

If you keep a stick of chalk in with your silver jewellery, it keeps it from tarnishing – it is also great for silver dinner services. My grandmother taught me this and it does work.

diamondsparkle

How to clean silver

Get a large bowl (or use the sink) and line the bottom with aluminium foil. Fill it with hot, hot water, add baking soda, and put in your silver pieces. The tarnish will come off the silver and stick to the aluminium foil all by itself – no need to scrub or anything. Works like a charm in just a couple of minutes.

lalaland

How to remove rust marks from chrome

Try tin foil scrunched up and rub away the rust – I tried it and it really worked!

animal2415

How to stop dogs fouling near your house

Not every dog owner picks poop up! Dilute some Jeyes fluid into an old watering can or a pump sprayer and spray around your property, local lamppost, and even your grass. The animals don't like the smell and will poop and pee elsewhere. Do it about twice a month.

carolec

How to stop a door from squeaking

If you don't have any oil or are worried about getting a mess on your carpet etc, try a tiny blob of washing up liquid on the hinges. It sounds bonkers but my gran has sworn by it for years and it really works!

saz57

How to remove a broken lightbulb

Take half an uncooked potato (the big, starchy kind). Stick it over the ragged lightbulb end to protect you from broken glass. Twist the lightbulb out of the socket.

rsjdooley

How to stop curtain tracks from sticking

If your curtains don't run smoothly on the curtain track, wipe the track with a little furniture polish. It works wonders.

Rosbod

How to clean leather furniture

If you are short of leather cleaner a baby wipe is excellent – if it's good enough for babies' bottoms it's good enough for leather.

housewifeandsuperstar

How to stop floorboards from creaking

If you dust talcum powder between the floorboards it sometimes stops them creaking.

Samantha

How to make drawers run more smoothly

If old wooden drawers are sticking, try rubbing the edges with old candles.

Bridget

How to stop sewing thread from tangling

If you knot the end that was closest to the reel, and thread the furthest end through your needle, it should stop tangling and knotting.

Mary

How to pick up broken glass

Use a wet piece of cotton wool; it should pick up even the tiny shards.

Noelle

Use a slice of fresh bread which easily picks up the smallest bits of broken glass.

Scarlett

Think there are still shards of glass that you might have missed? Shine a flashlight over the area. Any remaining glass should shimmer in the light.

Holly

How to fix screws in awkward places

Use Blu-Tack to stick the screw head to the screwdriver. This is brilliant in cases when gravity is against you, i.e. the screw has to go in upside down.

LevantineLass

How to remove soap scum from children's bath toys or keep it from building up

Put them into the dishwasher!

sk1970

How to clean hard-water stains from glass shower doors

To get rid of the stains I use lemon juice – the acid dissolves the lime scale. I also use a squeegee (used when washing and drying windows) to wipe the glass straight after showering to remove the water.

star

How to clean taps

Keep an old toothbrush with your cleaning kit, then every time you clean the basin or sink, use it to scrub round the base of the taps – much easier than trying to get a cloth in there, and it keeps the lime scale down.

Labink

Soak a piece of kitchen roll in white vinegar and wrap around base of taps. Leave for as long as possible – at least half an hour. Gets rid of lime scale like a dream.

karenannerichards

How to temporarily stop the annoying noise of a drip from a leaking tap

Tie dental floss around the end of the tap and let the floss tail hang into the bowl of the sink. Water will travel down the floss into the basin rather than dropping from the tap.

Tonya

How to wash glasses

Remember when hand-washing glasses that it's the outsides that get the finger and lipstick marks and need most attention; the insides are easy.

Cali

How to deodorise your microwave

Put in a bowl of water containing half a sliced lemon and cook on high for thirty minutes.

Rosa

How to clean a disgusting microwave

Put some washing up liquid into a jug of cold water, and put it in the microwave for three or four minutes, depending on just how disgusting it actually is. After the time is up, you will be able to wipe all the gunk off easily just using a cloth and some warm water.

Kate

How to clean your dishwasher

No need for expensive proprietary cleaners. Just put a handful of washing soda in the bottom of the dishwasher, set it on the hottest cycle, making sure the machine is empty of course, and go!

sandrak

How to keep your kitchen sponge from breeding bacteria

Put it in your dishwasher every time you run the dishes.

frankiegpizza

How to clean brushed stainless steel appliances

Clean first with a soft cloth and soapy water, then use baby oil on a cotton pad to polish it when dry.

tolgyesikara

How to clean drinking-glasses which have become cloudy, from the dishwasher

Adding baking soda to the water will take the cloudiness out.

pinkebo15

How to clean a knife block

Wrap a blunt-ended knife in an antibacterial wipe to clean the slots.

leggbarbara

How to remove Biro ink

Hairspray really gets rid of ballpoint ink. Just drench the mark with hairspray and you will see it start to lift off. Then rinse with cold water.

Mya

The best way to get rid of Biro or ink on clothing is to soak the stain in milk. Just pour some milk into a bowl and put the stained area in and make sure it is covered by the milk. Leave for as long as possible, overnight even, and then wash as normal and your stain will disappear.

LesleyJ

How to prevent pollen stains on fabrics

Don't go near them with water! Gently blow off any pollen, then roll some sticky tape around your fingers, and use the tape to gently dab off the pollen. Keep rotating the tape and dabbing until it all comes away.

NicoleS

Another good tip to prevent pollen disasters is, the moment your floral arrangement is in the vase, get some tissue and scissors and snip off the ends of the stamens into the tissue and toss in the bin – you can avoid the nasty stuff altogether.

eva123

How to get grease marks out of suede

Use fuller's earth – it's made of clay so it soaks those stains right up.

Rosa

How to clean suede

If you get a mark on suede, use a clean pencil eraser.

AnyaHindmarch

How to remove old sweat stains

If it's cotton, then soak the area in lots and lots of soluble aspirin in water. Wash as normal.

Caroline

Use a bucket (or the sink) of warm water with one cup of vinegar – white vinegar is great – and mix in. Soak your clothes for a couple of hours before laundering as usual. Do not use this method on dry-clean-only clothing.

iridescentfaith

How to stop pillow cases getting stained with face cream

If you really lightly starch your pillow cases it will help to prevent face creams staining them.

Jennifer

How to remove permanent-marker stains

Nail polish remover works for removing from skin, tables, etc.

brunettebombshell

How to get stains out of the carpet

Shaving foam is a great carpet cleaner.

Greer

How to remove stains from marble

You can remove stains from marble with a paste of baking soda, water and lemon juice. Rinse with plain water.

Maeve

How to remove blood from fabrics

If you dip the affected area in milk the blood stain will break down and will wash out on a normal cycle.

charleywilde

How to remove a red wine stain

Most solutions suggest either salt, soda water or splashing with white wine. Their effectiveness depends on the pungency of the red wine and whatever it has been spilled on. Always soak up any excess as quickly as possible, then sprinkle with salt before rinsing with cold water or soda water, which should flush most of the stain away. Then wash as usual. If you are particularly accident prone, perhaps invest in a specialist cleaner to have on stand-by!

nikkiwelch24

How to remove grass stains

Rub on plenty of treacle and afterwards wash the garment in tepid water.

Brittany

Cream of tartar mixed with water to a paste removes grass stains when brushed on and left to wash in the washing machine.

soobie

How to wash heavy linen and maintain a soft, fluid feel to the fabric

Use a cold wash with liquid detergent. Do NOT use fabric softener. Use the same amount of ordinary vinegar instead: it's good for the softness, holds colour and it descales your washing machine all in one! Use it for all your laundry and you'll notice the difference. Oh yes . . . your laundry will not smell like vinaigrette.

Georgio

How to make your laundry smell great

To infuse your own fragrance choice – use an unfragranced dryer sheet, lightly spray it with your favourite scent, and then toss in the dryer.

MARTE

How to dry a puffa jacket

Put a tennis ball into the dryer with down-filled objects to keep the down properly distributed.

Magnolia

Cars

or

I just want the damn thing to get me from A to B

How to retrieve things that slip down the sides of car seats

I always have a fondue fork to retrieve things from tight places. It is amazing the number of times I use it at home too!

MaryEllen

How to avoid static shock from the car after driving

Before you get out of the car, touch the door frame and then step out, but keep touching the metal while you put your feet on the ground. The electricity will be discharged.

JuliaM

How to get your car out when you're stuck in the mud, snow or ice

First try putting sticks, branches or the foot-well mats under the tyres for traction, then try letting a tiny bit of air out of your tyres.

Queenie

Keeping a bag of kitty litter in the boot of the car in the winter helps as well – spread it in front of the wheels to give you some traction on ice or mud.

suejak

How to remove dents

Before you admit to a prang you can always try pulling a small dent out of the bodywork with a toilet plunger.

Karen

How to clean oil off a driveway when detergent, bleach, scrubbing etc make no difference

Cola works. Simply pour it on the stain, leave for about one hour and wash it off with very hot water and a stiff brush.

asherlox

How to clean fresh oil off a driveway

If the oil spill is new, cat litter will absorb it. Just sprinkle enough to cover the oil stain, let it sit for a few days, and then sweep up the mess.

ramee151

How to save money on petrol

If you've turned your car into a giant storage bin and endlessly cart all sorts of junk around, clear it out! A heavier car uses more petrol.

Autumn

How to find your car again after parking

When you are parking in an unfamiliar area, use the camera on your phone to take a picture of the nearest street-name sign.

neets22

How to clean the inside of your car

If you tend to use drive-through car washes, you can give the inside a quick, effective clean at the same time. Keep a carrier bag with a packet of antibacterial wipes in your glove compartment so that you can empty all of your rubbish into the bag and give the inside of the car a quick wipe over with the wipes while you wait.

monkeyface

To clean the fiddly bits, like the joins in the dashboard and down round the gear stick, use a clean dry paintbrush. It gets into the cracks and lifts out the dust, which you can then wipe away.

Tatchull

How not to de-ice your windscreen

Whatever you do don't use salt on your windscreen. It will be splashed on to the paintwork which will rust very quickly. You've all seen the cars that live at the seaside.

pippinpuss

How to be organised if you have an accident

Always keep a cheap disposable camera in the glove compartment of your car (or use the camera on your phone) so that you can take a picture of the dent or other damage. This is also good if you get an unwarranted ticket and want to prove you were in the right.

LevantineLass

How to cope with pumping up tyres

Always keep a pair of disposable gloves in your glove compartment for when you need to check your tyre pressures to avoid getting your hands dirty.

sallyl

How to not pay too much for a car

Be prepared to walk away to go to another dealership. I did this twice and they came down in price. Also ask them to throw in some roof racks or other accessories as a bargaining chip . . . hey you can always ASK! I paid the price I wanted but without roof racks. I always regretted that.

jluich

How to freshen the way your car smells

I put tumble dryer sheets under the seats. Smell great, replace once a week.

0002mcl

Health and Fitness

or

Pizza is not an appropriate breakfast food

How to improve your balance and posture

Think of your nipples as headlights and keep them lighting the way ahead, not the road at your feet!

Yvonne

Adjust your desk chair so it sits as low as is still comfortable. This way, you are never tempted to slouch and you look straight ahead at the computer screen.

Brenna

How to get rid of a stye in your eyelid

This may seem really strange but I remember when I was very young, the older folks used to say to rub a gold ring over the stye. I don't know whether it was coincidence or not, but it worked.

nala

How to treat sunburn

Take an anti-inflammatory like ibuprofen, and then soak in a bath with a cupful of baking soda in it.

Shirley

Apply a few drops of lavender oil to cotton wool and spread over the skin – the burning sensation will lessen within half an hour and the burn will stay brown for longer.

Help123

Add some vinegar to cool water and wring out a tea towel in it. Just lay this on the sunburn. Really does work.

Redlady

How to stop smoking

I used the three-minute rule – when you feel a craving, say to yourself, I'll wait three minutes and then see how I feel. The craving always subsided after the three minutes were up, and I had usually been distracted by something else during the wait! Simple but effective, it got me through – it's six years since my last cigarette!

DawnRaid

How to de-stress

When really stressed in a situation, breathe in love and breathe out fear . . . it works!

ElleMacpherson

Try boxing. Beat the snot out of your least favourite pillow. If violence doesn't appeal to you, try any really heart-pumping cardio. Running and rowing both do it for me. Not only are you working too hard to stay stressed out, but the endorphins these activities create will make you feel better.

keryn

Stand up straight, put your hands at your side, lift them slowly up over your head and stretch as if you are trying to push the ceiling back in place. Then take a deep breath and exhale with a sigh three times.

Masi

How to eat more fruit

I freeze fresh fruit – blueberries and raspberries (I use Ziploc freezer bags) – then add the frozen berries to my cereal. It keeps the milk cold.

Bethany

How to remember to do pelvic floor exercises

If you have a slow internet connection or often wait for things to download, use this time to do pelvic floor exercises. You'd only be staring into space anyway.

Leah

Another idea is to do them after you've been to the loo – as most people go several times a day, you'll have them strengthened up in no time!

ella

I do them every time I stop for a traffic light, until it turns green. It will become a habit very quickly, once you see the quick results.

coleen

Do them whilst waiting at the bus stop! Nobody knows, which makes it quite entertaining too.

star

How to keep really cool in a hot climate

Put a damp cloth under your sun hat.

Verity

I live in Florida, AND I'm post-menopausal and have horrible hot flushes, so keeping cool is a priority with me. A quick cool-off that always works is to wet your hands with cool water, and gently rub the water on your arms and legs, the back of your neck, and your face. The rubbing will bring your blood to the surface, where the water will cool it (stand in front of a fan if possible). Also, wear cotton! Polyester and blends don't absorb moisture, and make you really hot.

asildem

How to help your partner lose weight

Instead of nagging him to go to the gym why don't you take up a sport that you can do together (and preferably involves a cute outfit for you) such as tennis. If you are a cunning woman you will let him be just a tiny bit better at the sport than you are.

Lucinda

How to get back to sleep

If you suffer from insomnia due to a racing brain, try counting your breaths. If you get distracted and find yourself thinking about something else, start again. You'll soon bore yourself to sleep.

Deborah

Think of a colour, and then think of all the things in the world that are that colour, and list them in your head . . . it's . . . sooo . . . boring . . .

bangzoom

Throw off the covers and get really really cold for about ten minutes or as long as you can stand, then turn on to your side and pull up the covers! Works every time.

joesaunt

How to dry up chicken pox

Bathe the victim twice a day in a bath loaded with Epsom salts.

Agnes

I found that bicarbonate of soda in the bath water helped to soothe and prevent scratching, or use Dead Sea salt, which has other minerals as well as the magnesium which must have helped in Epsom salts. Also, dabbing with good old calamine lotion will dry them out.

meeze

How to manage toothache

Instead of loading up on pills, try holding an ice cube on the bit of skin between your thumb and forefinger on the same side as your toothache's on. Don't leave it on for long or you'll get a 'burn'.

Carissa

If you cannot get hold of any ice easily, just try pinching the same piece of skin between the thumb and forefinger on the same side that your toothache is coming from.

rosepink

How to not catch a cold

Wash your hands A LOT – and stop touching your face. You pick up masses of germs by touching things and then touching your eyes, nose or mouth – these are all great entry points for germs.

Golda

How to ward off a chest cold

This works but must be applied with care. Spread a square of cotton or flannel with a thick paste made of water and mustard powder. Fold over and apply to the area around the collarbones so that the paste doesn't touch the skin, but the fumes can be breathed. Leave only for a minute or two as the skin can be burned and blister from the mustard.

Noelle

How to know how long you should brush your teeth for

If you want to know how long you should brush your teeth for, imagine singing 'Happy Birthday' to yourself twice over. It cheers the morning up no end. And you should get into the habit of doing pelvic floor exercises at the same time.

Kerry

How to remember to take pills

What works for me is putting the pill by my toothbrush. Or put it by something else you use everyday, like your makeup bag. It will jog your memory and help you take it at pretty much the same time each day.

livliv

I set 'Pills' as a daily event in the calendar on my mobile phone. That way the alarm will go off at the same time every day and I never forget.

bunny

How to stop a bee sting stinging

Once you have removed the sting, rub the area with a banana skin.

Scout

Don't know how this one works, but remove the sting and Sellotape a penny over where it was – it will stop hurting and the swelling and redness will go down in fifteen minutes.

Quintella

How to get rid of the sting from stinging nettles apart from using a dock leaf

Teething gel . . . this numbs the area.

pearldragon

Lashings of calamine lotion! Cools it down and stops it stinging. Great stuff!

sophie08

How to soothe a jellyfish sting

I find that rubbing the area with vinegar – any kind of vinegar – takes the sting away.

curvylady

How to remove a splinter

Put some hot water in a small jar and hold the top of the jar pressed over where the splinter is. You need to make it airtight and the splinter will be drawn out!

chrissie

A splinter comes out much more easily if you soak the whole area in olive oil first.

Mallory

How to avoid eye injuries

Always strike matches away from you. A flying ember in the eye is not fun.

Rain

How to stop muscle cramps

When you get cramp in your calf, stretch your leg out and pull your foot up so it's at a sort of right angle with your leg. It goes straightaway!

leighanneb18

If you get a cramp in your calf, the best thing to do is stand facing a wall and lean forward against it, heels still on the ground, so you are really stretching out your calf muscle.

Leah

How to keep to an exercise plan

Schedule exercise appointments in your diary, so you actively block out the time for them. If you try to just fit them in where you can, everything else will take priority.

Winifred

How to exercise for free

Take a pair of trainers to work with you and keep them under your desk. Go for a lunchtime walk three times a week with your ipod, and then grab a sandwich on the way back, and you'll still have your evenings free to spend with family/friends. I usually go for a forty-minute walk. Wrap up warmer in winter and wear a hat.

claireg

If you travel to work by bus, get off one stop before you usually do, and walk the rest of the way. This can gradually be increased to two stops. Also, walk up and down stairs instead of using the lift. You can start by doing up stairs for a week, and then down, and then combine both.

Finlandia

How to keep fit without the gym

I have a routine of exercises I do at home which target the areas I want to tone – i.e. sit-ups, leg raises, lifting weights, stretches, etc – each for the duration of a CD or radio track. I change exercise for each track. I've tried various exercise videos/CDs and never stuck to them. Every week I'll change my programme slightly. If I don't do it one day, then I'll double up next day. This takes me no longer than twenty minutes (I'm basically lazy). After nearly a year of this, I have a much more defined waistline, toned arms and shoulders, and my bottom is starting to defy gravity again. I no longer have the expense or guilt of gym membership that I can't be arsed to go to.

Julie1533

How to tone up your bum

Squeeze your buttocks while watching TV – do it very quickly, around fifty at a time.

Redlady

How to tone your tummy

Start first thing in the morning: breathe properly and hold your tummy in while you brush your teeth, get dressed, have breakfast. It will become a habit.

Luz

Sit up straight, pull your stomach in as far as it can go, hold and count backwards from one hundred. It's harder than think, but if you work up to doing this eight times a day you'll see the difference.

Masi

How to look good with a hangover

The key is (weirdly) to wear less makeup, rather than trying to disguise the effects with more. Your skin will be dehydrated, so moisturise vigorously. Cover up under-eye bags with a light touch, put a bit of healthy-looking pink blusher on the apples of your cheeks, stick to sheer and pale eye shadows and apply mascara – if your hand isn't shaking too much.

Sharon

Wear a crisp, white shirt with a collar. It will reflect light on to your face and no one will be any the wiser! I used to always keep an ironed shirt in the wardrobe for such emergencies . . . nothing shows up your hangover quite like a crumpled black shirt.

jennpod

I have a friend who applies a light fake-tan moisturiser last thing before bed at the end of a big night and wakes up looking sun-kissed and healthy.

Blingrid

Diets

or

Anything you eat standing up doesn't count, anything liquid
doesn't count, and broken cookies don't count because
all the calories leak out

How to stick to a diet

Stop beating yourself up. You will 'cheat'. Most people start a diet, cheat
and then say, 'That's it! The diet's over for good.' Instead, acknowledge
that you made an error and make a U-turn. Have you ever been in a car
with a GPS system? If you miss a turn does the computer say, 'You (fat)
idiot! I can't believe you missed that turn (ate 57 cookies!)' No, the
computer says, 'Please make a U-turn.' No judgments, just a gentle
instruction. Dieters must do this as well.

sandrasimmons

Like a recovering alcoholic, take it one day at a time. Say to yourself,
'For today, I won't eat any chocolate.' It's far less scary than thinking
you'll never eat chocolate ever again, and as the days pass it will become
a habit. And there's nothing more habit-forming than habit.

Natalie

How to make your weekly chocolate bar treat last longer

OK, don't you hate it when your Mars bar treat (which you allow yourself during your diet) is scoffed down so fast that you can't even taste it? Well, an easy solution to this is to freeze the Mars bar first, then when you go to eat it you have to really suck on it and defrost it to taste it! Problem solved, no cals added! Long-lasting, and more of a chocolate high for you!

seksykt

How to loose weight by eating

A friend of mine told me her aunt lost sixty pounds in a year by simply eating what she wanted to, but splitting the meal in half. So basically anything she would normally eat she only consumed half and cut down on calories!!

Palacinka

How to stop yourself boredom munching at night

When the telly's rubbish all you feel like doing is eating, right? Well what I do is give myself a manicure – you can't eat with wet nails! You'll stay slim and get gorgeous nails. Even if you're rubbish at nails it doesn't matter. Good luck.

blondiesuz

Knit! You can't eat whilst knitting – and messy fingers make for messy yarn, so you can't even nibble and knit alternately. Even if all you're capable of is good old plain stitch, you can liberate all your friends' leftover wool and knit small squares which you can then stitch up into a lovely sofa blanket for cold nights or chilly mornings.

PoshPaws

How to painlessly curb your appetite

Prepare hard-boiled eggs in advance and just have them around. Also, steamed vegetables, when cold, are delicious. Much easier if you just get into the habit of making them and leaving them to be picked at.

LevantineLass

Drink water! I keep a small bottle of water at my desk and drink it all day long. The small bottle is key because it doesn't seem like an overwhelming amount, plus it gets you off your bum to refill it at the water cooler down the hall!

rgmontgomery

How to feel full for longer and stop cravings for sweet things

A really big breakfast seems to do it for me. Porridge is almost impossible to beat and very healthy too. Also healthy and filling are a couple of boiled eggs and wholewheat toast.

Alice

How to eat less

Use the smallest cutlery you can, e.g. a teaspoon instead of a dessertspoon; it makes you think you're eating more.

Bijou

It's really simple – always put your knife and fork down while chewing. It makes you eat WAY more slowly and therefore you feel fuller having eaten less.

Marina

The appetite is stimulated by different flavours, so say to yourself, 'If I'm still really hungry I can have more of what I just ate, instead of a pudding.' If that isn't so appealing you know you're just being greedy. In fact, a good way to eat less is to eat just a big plate of all one thing – you'll bore yourself into submission.

Jennifer

How to work out why you aren't losing weight

Keep a diary of every single thing you put in your mouth, including drinks. It can be kind of scary how quickly it adds up.

Indira

How to stop the snacking

Instead of three large meals, eat fist-size meals every three hours. Spread your calorific intake over six meals instead of three. Include a small piece of protein with each meal. You will never feel hungry. I lost 10kg by doing this.

laureah21

How to speed up your metabolism

Strength training builds muscle mass, which activates your metabolism. Muscle is an active tissue, and it's the engine that will rev up your metabolism. That's because muscle burns more calories than fat. Building muscle is the most fundamental component in staying lean. Think of muscle and metabolism working together, like a partnership. The more muscle tissue you have, the higher your metabolism and the more calories you'll burn when you rest. The less muscle you have, the less calories you'll burn. The best way to get your metabolism to work faster, so that you can burn more calories, is by building more muscle – lifting weights and strength training. Losing weight doesn't happen just by eating little and doing some cardio; that plan can actually slow down your metabolism. One pound of muscle burns seventy-five calories, while one pound of fat burns two calories.

selfinthecity

How to stop worrying about your body image

Make a list of things that you like about yourself – and not just the physical things. Are you just your body or do you value your other assets? When you think of the things you don't like about your body are they things that you can change with diet and exercise? Think of three people you admire: is it only their bodies you find attractive? Your body is always a work in progress – worry about keeping your heart open and your mind alert.

Masi

Beauty

or

They said that spots were just a phase. They lied

How to do DIY waxing

If you are going to wax yourself, be committed to it. Don't kid yourself.
It will hurt. Pulling slowly, or less violently, will not make it less painful.
It will just pull off skin, or cause irritation. Be committed to ripping it
off, despite the sound of ripping carpet and feeling of pain.

Slothie

Make sure you hold down the skin at the bottom of the wax strip so that
the area you are ripping wax off is taut. This will ensure the strip is
pulled off quicker without taking half your leg or bikini area with it!

Hussy

How to prepare for a bikini wax

Exfoliate and scrub like your life depends on it for a week before your
appointment. Do it on the day of the wax as well and you'll be set. Plain
cotton underwear is a girl's best friend.

TraceyMichelle

Take a painkiller an hour before and it won't hurt as bad.

pklimas

How to relatively painlessly wax your upper lip

This is a tip and a half I got from my mum, when I started waxing. Rub a bit of Bonjela into your upper lip, so that it's absorbed. Then wash off the excess and pat dry – your skin should feel curiously detached from your face. Then wax away as you normally would. It still hurts a bit, but not as badly as previously and you feel a lot more committed to doing it.

Slothie

How to beat shaving rash

Buy a big bottle of light conditioner for hair. Use it in the shower to shave your legs. It works better than shaving foam or soap, and leaves your legs soft and smooth.

maresydotes

Shaving your legs last thing in the shower allows the skin and hair to soften and helps to prevent razor burn. This works with soap, conditioner or shaving cream!

pinkebo15

I find the most vital part of shaving overall is exfoliating. I used to get terrible shaving rash all over, which I then realised was due to my dry skin. My razor would snag on it and I tried everything. Eventually I got so fed up with it that I bought a sugar rub, which you can get from most beauty shops or supermarkets, then would exfoliate like mad to make sure my legs were as smooth as could be before shaving. Since this my legs have been silky smooth, and exfoliating also prevents ingrown hairs. Trust me on this one, girls. Exfoliating is possibly the best thing you can do for your skin. Keeps the skin fresh.

Irishcharm

How to get the best result with fake tan

Slather your hands, elbows, knees and feet with moisturiser before you
apply fake tan. Immediately afterwards wash your hands thoroughly and
wipe your knees, elbows, ankles and backs of your knees.

Abigail

How to stop fake tan staining your sheets

If you've just applied fake tan and don't want to stain your sheets, get
an old duvet cover and simply sleep inside it with your duvet on top.
(I always take one when I have to sleep in hotels that could be cleaner
too.)

Bianca

How to get rid of fake tan streaks

Apply whitening toothpaste to the dark area for a short while . . . wash it
off and you'll see it diminishes the colour. This is also very effective if
you've applied fake tan with bare hands and now have orange palms.
Applying whitening toothpaste liberally to your palms for five minutes
solves the problem!

Barrkas

Nail varnish remover works!

nominoo

I found (accidentally) that cream hair bleach will remove self-tan. Since
it's so thick, it can be placed exactly where you want it. Just leave it on a
couple of minutes, testing to see if it's worked its magic. Then I go over
the area with self-tan mixed with moisturiser for a softer, blended tan
line.

mcat35

How to make little boobs or no-boobs look a little bigger and more obvious

Brush some bronzer between the top of your boobs to give the illusion of a bigger cleavage.

Princess21

How to make your own body scrub

Granulated sugar mixed with your body wash or shampoo makes an amazingly cheap and effective body scrub. I tried it and now have a glass container of sugar in my bathroom. It works better than anything I've ever tried before. I have a really foamy face wash, so use it with that and it lathers up and scrubs leaving me super soft and smooth, without oil! I apply my own oil afterwards so it doesn't leave my bath all greasy.

Halle

How to prevent backne

Put a few drops of tea tree oil in your bath water every day. The result? AMAZING! I have suffered back acne all my life – after this my back is flawless.

obaseme

When showering, always wash/condition/rinse hair first and then wash your back. If you don't wash it off the residue from your hair will stay on your back and cause spots.

kated

How to clean out clogged pores and blackheads

Make a paste using baking soda and a little water. It should be fairly thick, but moist. Use the paste as a scrub to exfoliate clogged pores. Works like a charm!

amandag

How to improve your skin

Wash your face with honey! Use pure honey (raw organic if you can get it) and just smooth a little on and rinse off. This can clear up acne and blackheads and is all natural. It's also anti-microbial and tastes good, too!

ZenMomma

It smells awful, but apple cider vinegar brings a radiant glow to your face! Don't use this to leave the house or sleep next to your boy, but apply with a cotton ball when you can escape being sniffed out. I've also made a cleanser with honey, salt, and apple cider vinegar. Exfoliating, peeling, hydrating. Awesome.

vaportrailed

How to make a cheap acne/exfoliation solution

Use uncoated aspirin. Place four or five tablets in a small container and mix with about a teaspoon of warm water to create a paste. Apply to the skin and let dry for fifteen to twenty minutes. When removing, lightly rub the skin (exfoliate) in a circular motion until the paste is removed. Rinse with warm water. The result is baby-soft skin. Cost less than £1.00. Use this also to dry out pimples individually.

PS. This is very drying to the skin. Be sure to tone and moisturise. Do not overuse. Once a week is perfect.

aboutface22

How to stop your knees and elbows ageing before the rest of you

Watch your elbows. Elbows, necks and hands are the quickest things to age. When you've put your night cream on, rub what's left on your hands on your elbows.

Tracy

How to look after a new tattoo

I think the best solution is definitely Sudocrem – I know it's meant for nappy rash but the thick texture and the antiseptic in it are really good. Also, use arnica cream around the tattoo if you have had it done in a 'bony' place like a shoulder.

charke

How to beat cellulite

Don't get mad at your cottage cheese thighs, pamper them. Get a great-smelling moisturiser with skin-tightening properties, and use it daily. And remember that the lighter your skin, the more your least favourite dimples will show. So consider a self-tanner for a little camouflage! Exercise, and drink water. Love yourself, dimples and all!

ListenGirlies

I work in a gym so I kind of know what's great and what's rubbish and a machine called a stepper is fantastic and about the best you can get for your bum. If you can manage ten minutes every two days on that I guarantee miracles in a couple of weeks. A tan can also help cover it.

tink

Don't try to beat cellulite – get over it. Anyone who judges you by the dimpliness of your thighs isn't worth the bother, and cellulite can't be got rid of anyway. You can improve it for a short while, but it is just the body's way of storing fat – in little pockets. Sorry gals!

littlebean

How to keep your breasts perky as long as possible

I am sixty-three and have really perky breasts. I spray them daily with cold water and do the following exercise: clasp hands together and push, do around fifty repetitions.

Redlady

How to have sexy kissable lips

With or without lipstick, the key is smooth, non-chapped lips. Easiest and quickest way to smooth out chapped lips is to use vitamin E capsules which can be purchased from a chemist or health food store. The capsules are meant to be swallowed, but instead cut one open at night and apply the liquid to your lips (there will be more than enough – use the left-over liquid on your cuticles!). The fastest way to unchapped lips ever!

DezG

The key to sexy, kissable lips is to bite them (not hard!) every so often. This will send blood to them and plump them out without any glosses. It will definitely make you look like Angelina!

BodyEnvy

How to cover up a hickey (love bite)

Don't just cover up a hickey . . . get rid of it! The trick is to really really scrub it . . . as if you are trying to scrub it right off your skin. Either get a face wash and warm water, or hop in a warm shower and give it a really good rub. I know, I know . . . I thought, What the . . .! BUT IT REALLY WORKS.

blueintrinsic

How to beat dry feet

If you have really thick, dry skin on your feet, you need to scrub them. You can find amazing foot files, like something you'd find in a toolbox, which scrape off so much dry skin! Soak your feet in warm water for five minutes, then scrape off all the dry skin. This will make the moisturiser work better.

lisa85

How to stop cracked heels

Lather your feet at bedtime with good old Vaseline, with extra coverage on the heels. Put on cotton socks and the next morning your feet are like a baby's.

Lucille

How to get rid of yellow skin on the soles of feet

Get a tomato and cut off the top, the part you usually throw away. Then rub it over your callouses – the citric acid will soften them. You need to do it a few times to see results, but it's less dangerous than using a blade.

Masi

How to look and feel great

You don't need a PhD for this one girls, or guys for that matter. It's simple! All you have to do is SEE – Sleep+Exercise+Eat healthily.

sjmundy

How to deal with unshaven legs in the bedroom, and no time to deal with it

Wear stockings – under a skirt. He probably won't mind you keeping them on!

buddha

How to whiten teeth without harsh chemicals

Brush your teeth with strawberries. Mash a couple in a small pot so the juice and flesh is exposed. Use your toothbrush to apply.

Clio

How to get food out of your teeth when you're nowhere near a toothbrush

It may sound gross, but if you're stuck with nothing to use, the post or wire of an earring will work. You can clean it later in the bathroom, or use hand sanitiser on it before reinserting.

pmc1720

How to apply perfume

Apply perfume once you have washed and moisturised. However, always try to remember this strict rule . . . if you can still smell your perfume a couple of minutes after applying it, you're wearing too much!

sophie08

My mate found out that the bloke at work she fancied liked Jean Paul Gaultier on women. So when she was ironing all her work shirts she poured tiny amount of perfume into the iron where the water goes. Her shirts had a very subtle whiff of Jean Paul, and the bloke was entranced as she obviously hadn't doused herself in the stuff. He couldn't work out why she smelt so heavenly. The iron was probably ruined, but she said the attention was worth it from said man.

ishouldjojo

How to immediately brighten your eyes

Using white or pale, pale blue eye shadow, dab a bit of shadow in a sideways 'V' around the inner corner of each eye. Your eyes will look bright and wide-awake! Shadow works better than liner or eye pencil – much subtler.

CeeVee

How to avoid eye infections

Don't rub your eyes. I read somewhere that your hands/fingers are germy. Thus, don't rub your eyes. As a person with a nervous habit of rubbing my eyes, it took me two pink-eyes and a puffy right eye to finally get it through my thick head to stop.

hummer

How to know what shape to pluck your eyebrows

If you've got thick eyebrows, and you want to know what the plucked shape will look like, take a white eyeliner pencil and draw over the hairs you're going to take off, and that will give you an indication.

Gwendolen

You can also usually tell by looking at the top line of your eyebrow. That is always the sort of shape that suits your face.

minxi

When to pluck your eyebrows
Pluck before you go to bed, NOT before you go out.

Tamsen

How to reduce the pain of plucking or waxing eye brows
To minimise the ouch factor of tweezing your eyebrows do this: press a hot flannel on to your eyebrows for a few minutes before plucking and the pain won't be as bad.

Hw92

How to have gorgeous eyebrows
Don't pluck your eyebrows at the top, always pluck from the bottom. It's usually best to get a professional to do them for you first, and then you can just pluck the new hairs as they grow Also, use strong bright light or daylight and a magnifying mirror. That way you can get all those hairs you don't normally see.

waxy1086

You can tame rogue eyebrows for the day by spraying a little hairspray on an old toothbrush and then grooming them with that. (Trying to spray hairspray directly on to your eyebrows is a terrible idea for all sorts of reasons.)

Twila

How to maintain eyelash curlers
The rubber on eyelash curlers cracks sometimes, and if you haven't noticed you'll cut your eyelashes right off. They can be like a guillotine. Turn the rubber around or buy a new pair.

Bridget

How to have a long-lasting curl for your eye lashes

Heating your eyelash curlers with a hairdryer first makes them far more effective – kind of like a mini curling tong – but always test the heat of the curlers on the back of your hand first though . . .

Daphne

If you do not have eyelash curlers, or do not like using them, then this is a tried and tested tip: brush on the mascara then, using your forefinger, hold edge of finger under lashes and gently push up and hold until dry

kimberly I

How to get an eyelash out of your eye without touching it

Just blow your nose with your eyes closed and your lids will water it out.

Weezy

How to bring down those puffy eyes

Put a cold teabag on each eye (store a few with a few drops of water in a sealable container in the fridge for easy access). Remove once the teabag warms up.

TraceyMichelle

Use two cotton wool pads dunked and slightly squeezed out in cold water. If they start to warm up, dunk them again. Keep them cold and on your eyes for around fifteen minutes, and, when you take them off, your eyes will feel refreshed and the puffiness will be no more. Also, when you go to sleep have lots of pillows so that your head is raised. The fluid that makes puffiness won't be able to get to your face as easily, so when you wake up your eyes will be less puffy than usual.

faerieeebaby

Which washing powder to use for sensitive skin

My boyfriend has very sensitive skin and we used to be able to use only non-bio washing powder, otherwise his skin would become itchy and sore. But even the perfume in that causes a reaction, especially when we wash our bed linen and towels, so now I use Eco Balls (you can buy them online – just enter Eco Balls on to Google). They're brilliant. You use them instead of fabric washing powder and conditioner and they last you up to one thousand washes! They don't contain any chemicals so will not react with your skin or the environment!

sophie08

How to take the red out of a spot

You can temporarily take the worst of the redness out of a spot with whitening eye drops.

Olwen

Use lavender oil; it really does calm down the redness. Just a drop overnight will do the trick.

patstanley

Green concealer is the best thing I have ever found for taking the red out of a spot!

pms1882

How to clear up spots

Frador – originally an ulcer treatment (available at all good pharmacies) – is a great quick-fix spot treatment! It dries them out super fast, to leave you looking great for that Saturday night out!

alicec

I highly recommend Sudocrem. It's gentle enough to use on babies' bottoms and is great for clearing up spots or acne. Put on a thin layer at night and you'll notice a big difference in only a few days. It costs a couple of pounds for a big pot. You'll find it in the baby section of most supermarkets and chemists.

katy81

My mum discovered Germolene for spots and I've been using it for years now. It works best on those horrible whitehead spots. It's so cheap, and doesn't dry your skin out like other acne or spot medication either.

livliv

How to moisturise at a low cost

My nan never used conventional moisturiser. Her remedy was: cut a large potato in half, rub the potato over your face and neck and leave until the starchy moisture has dried. Your face will feel a little bit crusty but not tight. Leave it for five minutes and rinse off with cool water. Her skin was magnificent up until she died at eighty years of age. I must confess I don't use the same method all the time, but I have used it often as it makes the skin feel very plump and refreshed.

Mandy

Lie in a very hot bath with a liberal application of extra virgin olive oil on your face. Let the face steam for thirty minutes and watch the lines vanish. Only lasts a few hours, but perfect for a night out.

higgy

Use petroleum jelly at night before sleeping (Vaseline for instance). It's cheap, it's not harsh, and leaves skin very moisturised. It can be used on the face, body, hands and feet!

sparkle99

How to deal with a shiny face

Instead of using expensive cosmetic blotting papers to get that matt look, try Rizla cigarette papers. They do exactly the same thing and are much cheaper!

Ottalie

How to prevent crow's feet

Always wear sunglasses on bright days to prevent squinting. Have your eyes tested regularly (yearly if over forty) for the same reason.

leggbarbara

How to make your own face-mask for oily skin

Buy a small box of fuller's earth from any chemist: you'll probably need to ask for it. It's really cheap and the box lasts ages. All you do is mix a few teaspoonsful with a little water, make a paste and spread it over your face and neck. It's a brilliant facial mask, and most masks in the shop have a base of this anyway.

toptip

How to get softer skin cheaply

If your skin is dry (especially winter legs), after bathing or showering massage liquid paraffin on your skin (most chemists have it). It's an ingredient in lots of skin creams and this is the only one you really need. Soft paraffin is also brilliant for cradle cap.

doingmybest

Use baby oil on damp skin (after a shower) and rub in well.

baby17

How to stop 'aeroplane skin'

Pick up a free sample of a face mask at the beauty counter when you pass by (look for a colourless one). It's small (so it will get around the airline restrictions), cheap, and easy to carry in your handbag. Clean and exfoliate your face before you leave your house, then, once you are in your seat, use a face wipe to clean off any airport grime and apply the face mask. Leave on for the entire flight, drink a lot of water, wrap yourself up in a pashmina to stay cosy, and get some sleep. Wipe off the face mask on arrival and you have had a great facial.

Amelia

Makeup

or

How can it take so long to make it look like I'm not wearing any?

Where to find good-quality makeup brushes without paying the earth for them

This is what I do, I go to the art supply shop. You can get different textures and sizes and you can test them against your skin if you are sensitive. I use a small rounded paintbrush for my foundation, and I have several different ones for concealer. You can even find an ultra thin one for eyeliner.

Masi

How to clean makeup brushes

Use a gentle shampoo. Do not wash where the hair joins the handle, otherwise it will loosen the glue. After washing, take a towel and press out any excess water. Lie the brush flat on a surface, such as a table, with the hair part exposed to air, so it can air dry. This is crucial for the brush to dry thoroughly and in its shape. You do not need to wash your own brushes more than once a month, if only you are using them.

Replicant

Add bicarbonate of soda to warm water and wash brushes as normal with a baby-washing product. Then rinse them well and towel dry. The bicarbonate of soda helps to loosen and dissolve any stubborn grease and makeup – and removes any unwanted odours! Works wonders every time.

Kezabell

How to wash makeup sponges

Use the net bags you get with washing powder tablets to contain your makeup sponges while they are in the washing machine.

sgrimwade

How to get rid of all eye makeup

Vaseline! It dissolves all mascaras (even waterproof), eyeliners, and eye shadows! Make sure it's warm so that it's soft and doesn't drag. Afterwards make sure to wipe away all traces with cotton wool.

nobodylikesasmartass

I have used baby oil for years – it gets rid of any mascara and it's very cheap. Just put some on a tissue and wipe gently. It also doesn't dry the skin. However, if you want to reapply mascara immediately afterwards, you need to wash off the baby oil first, otherwise you end up with big 'Panda-eyes'!

Anita123

How to apply false eyelashes

Glide them down – you're attaching them to the base of the lashes that are already there, not to your skin.

Magda

Let the glue almost dry so it's tacky before you put them on; if it's too wet they will slide around.

Verity

How to create a jaw line

If you're very careful you can use bronzer to sculpt your face a bit. Brush a little under your jaw line – but take it easy!

Makenzie

How to apply bronzer

Use a big brush and put it where the sun would hit your face – top of the cheekbones, brow bone, forehead, nose and chin. The point is to look as if you're sun-kissed, not coloured in. And don't forget your collarbone.

Larissa

How to organise your cosmetics drawer

Attach a piece of elastic to the inside of one of your drawers with thumb tacks. You can then slot all your lipsticks and various small tubes behind it, and they will stop rolling around.

Jane

Put a cutlery tray in your makeup drawer.

Magiwyn

How to deal with thin lips

Sorry, but unless you go to a plastic surgeon, they'll always be thin. Don't be tempted to colour them in bold and bright colours, it will only draw attention to their lack of volume. Instead, use pale and natural colours and sheer glosses.

Noreen

How to get the most out of a tube of cream

When you think your tube of cream has finished, cut the top off and look inside. You will find you still have loads left. You can always use a bulldog clip to keep the top sealed, or put the cut-off tip over the opening.

waxy1086

How to apply makeup

Especially for daytime, apply your makeup while facing the strongest source of natural daylight you can find. It's amazing how many women put their makeup on in inadequate light and go round looking like a clown all day. And don't forget to BLEND ladies!

Phoebe

How to keep lipstick on longer

Apply liner and lip colour as usual. Blot, then dab on a neutral pressed powder, followed by another layer of the lipstick. Blot again, and your favourite colour will last for hours.

KellyM

How to stop mascara smearing

Lightly powder over the eye area using a brush and loose neutral powder before applying mascara. This blots excess oil and helps thicken lashes.

leggbarbara

How to use blusher

Smile, then apply the blusher first to the apples of your cheeks. Blend to soften the colour until it looks natural. For a more sculpted look, suck cheeks in making a 'fish face' and sweep a non-shimmery bronzer or slightly darker foundation in the hollows of your cheeks before applying blusher. Blend!

patriciao

How to add instant glamour

Use individual false eyelashes – they are the easiest way to add instant glamour to any face. If they're too long and it looks a bit extreme, cut them with nail scissors – before you put them on.

Holly

How to not get lipstick on your teeth

After applying lipstick wrap a tissue around your index finger, put finger in your mouth and shut your mouth to blot lipstick. Then smile – always works. Remember to remove finger before smiling.

noeleblue

How to choose the right foundation

Test your foundation on your jaw line and not your hand to make sure it matches your skin tone.

Hw92

Find the two shades that come closest, buy them both and mix them at home every day. You'll be able to readjust the pigment level to match your natural colour which can change from day to day anyway.

Masi

Nails

Or

How hard can it be to keep them looking nice?
Oh yes, I remember . . .

How to paint toenails easily

To avoid being a contortionist I have found the best way to paint my toenails is to sit on the stairs. My feet are instantly raised nearer to me on the steps below so that I can easily reach them and maintain my balance.

Linx

Paint those toes with wild abandon! Just do it in the evening so they can dry completely before you go to sleep. In the morning shower any polish slopped on your skin will practically wipe away.

blazabla

How to perfect a pedicure

Your toenails may look fab, but I'm betting your toes don't! Right before you get into the shower, dip a cotton swab into baby oil and run the swab over the cuticles, sides and top of each toe. Repeat for each toe. The heat of the shower helps the oil sink in and you'll emerge with perfectly varnished nails AND healthy toes that don't look dry or scaly.

CeeVee

How to apply nail polish without streaks

I apply a base coat first. It evens out the nail and prepares it for the coloured nail varnish. Wait until it is completely dry (not tacky) and then paint your nails with one straight line going from the base to the tip on either side and then another down the middle. Re-dip the brush if you find it dragging along the nail. Some nail varnishes will always leave a streak – these are the two-tone ones which have a metallic under-tone. Try sticking to block colours.

sophie08

How to take care of a snaggly nail with no nail file

I always carry a matchbook in my purse. This way, I have matches if I need them (rarely!) and can also use the scratchy edge to file a snaggly nail if I can't find a nail file (all the time!).

CeeVee

The cement between bricks on a wall or any kind of rough wall works pretty well.

kakeiley

How to maintain a great manicure

Keep a nail file in the car, one in your handbag, and basically everywhere, so one is always handy if you find yourself at a loose end for a few minutes.

SamanthaCameron

How to quickly fix your manicure

If you have somehow managed to chip your nail varnish (as we all do . . . all the time!!) dip the affected nail into a capful of nail varnish remover. Literally dip it in and pull it straight back out again. Don't touch it with anything – leave it to dry (tip downwards). This smoothes out the chipped end. Once it's dry, run your finger over it to make sure that it's smooth . . . if not, repeat. You can then paint straight over! Voilà!

sophie08

How to cure a nail infection

Methylated spirits. Just apply to (in my case) toenails with cotton wool every day. I was desperate, but it seems to be working.

Carolyn10

If you get a nail fungus – or when your nails have had polish on for too long and have spots – soak them in Vicks Vapour Rub.

MelissaOdabash

How to tackle very dry or chapped hands

Use foot cream! I usually have really chapped, dry and cracking hands, but I've found that cracked heel repair cream really works on smoothing them out! It's very thick and creamy so it's good to use it at night or at least once a day. It really helped. The backs of my hands also looked younger and my usually flaky and crappy palms, fingers and cuticles look and feel almost normal now!

pjamas10

How to grow healthy and long nails

Take folic acid supplements. After two years of constantly flaking nails, I've taken folic acid for three months and have strong healthy nails again at last.

Cali

How to stop biting your nails

Have those synthetic tips put on for a week; you can't bite them and it gets you out of the habit. Then have the synthetic nails properly manicured and varnished – it'll put you right off.

Vivian

These are a couple of ways I stopped. First, I ALWAYS had polish on them. That made me stop completely. Second, I just think about where my fingers have been, and what could possibly be under my fingernails. I don't think most people clean their nails before they bite them! I just get grossed out by thinking about what could be there! Skin cells, dirt, old food particles and other stuff like that. Yuck. Plus, I don't want my hands to look ugly!

BodyEnvy

How to whiten nails

Denture cleaner – get two bowls of warm water (large enough to soak a hand in); add to each bowl one of those fizzy, denture-cleaning tablets; put a hand in each bowl and soak for at least fifteen minutes. Just as the denture cleaners work on stained false teeth, they whiten and brighten nails, too.

DezG

Use an old toothbrush and whitening toothpaste, preferably one of the slightly abrasive ones. Brush gently under your nails and leave on for a minute if you have time. Voilà!

patsharp

Dating

or

Do I like him? Does he like me? Do I have food in my teeth?

How to meet men

Hanging out in a DIY shop and asking a guy for advice about which drill to buy has always worked well. Of course I return the drill the next day. If I didn't, I'd have a drill for every night that I had a date during the summer of 2003.

Masi

Avoid being the princess in the tower and appearing unapproachable. Smile and be able to stand alone for a while – no one is ever going to approach anyone in a big gaggle of girls.

Helen

How to turn down someone who is asking you out when you are not interested – without lying

Put yourself in the guy's shoes. Don't be cruel and don't burn any bridges. Someone that you think you have nothing in common with today could be the man of your dreams in two years. People change. Always thank him for asking and tell him you are flattered but . . .

– I'm really busy these days.

– I'm not sure we have anything in common.

– let's not do anything we'll both regret.

Masi

How to get a guy's attention

OK, ignore all the women who are full of themselves and tell you to push your boobs and arse out! It's all a load of rubbish. The two things that a man notices about a woman are her mouth (whether or not she's smiling), then her eyes (whether or not she's keeping eye contact). So from this I suggest keep on smiling at him, sweetly and not in a creepy way! And try to keep subtle eye contact, again not in a creepy way! Also a laugh normally attracts male attention, if you laugh out loud at a joke etc (not at nothing, or he'll be getting the straitjacket out.) It shows that you're outgoing and fun, which men love. Try these things and I'm sure he'll be paying you all the attention you deserve.

seksykt

How to let a man know when you fancy him

If you've just spotted him, solid eye contact and a smile . . . if you've the courage!

hbkt83

How to be safe on dates

Watch for inconsistent behaviour and the bondage grip, where someone grabs your wrist in a way that throws you off balance. Don't give out too much information about yourself in the first six dates. Always carry your mobile phone with an ICE (In Case of Emergency) number programmed into it. Let your best friend know when you are going on a first date and have her call you – just in case you want to ditch him. And even if you think he's a keeper, call your BF when you go to the ladies room and let her know where you are.

Masi

How to see if you have food in your teeth without leaving the table

Discreetly use the blade of your knife as a mirror

Emily

How to eat on a date

In my experience, men like women who aren't afraid of food. Eat what you like! Good food is one of life's greatest pleasures, and if he disapproves of you eating too much bread or going for dessert on your first date, then he's going to make you miserable in the long run.

Shepherdess

How to offer to split the bill on a date

What I always do is let the guy ask for the bill (this can sometimes take a while if he isn't assertive). When he is given it, say casually, 'Right, what's the damage?' If he is going to split it with you, he'll tell you how much; if he isn't, then he'll say that's he's getting it. Only protest once. Say, 'Are you sure?' and leave it at that. I'm not a money-grabber, but I have usually found that guys who insist on paying on a first date are going to be better boyfriend material than guys who are happy to split the bill.

star

How to know for sure if he likes you

I've definitely found that if a guy likes you he will invariably find a way to tell you. If he's not interested, he won't make any special effort to speak to you, or hang out with you. It really is that simple.

nikkiwelch24

How to not put men off

If a guy comes back to your house with interior design, there is nothing worse than making your home too girly. Bin the teddy bears, avoid lace. It scares them.

Kendra

How to contact a man after a first date

You should not be contacting him!! He should be the one doing all the chasing! However, if you haven't heard from him in three or four days, send him a text such as 'Hey, just want to say thanks again for a lovely time on_____. We should do it again some time.' If you do not hear from him afterwards in two or three days, move on. If he is not chasing you, then he is not worth bothering about – you can do better.

Lynz

How to stop yourself calling him

What I do, though not always successfully, is change his name in my mobile address book to 'Don't', or to something appropriate to whatever crime I feel he's committed, e.g. 'inconsiderate bastard who cancelled at the last minute'.

annalouisa

If you have his number programmed into your phone, but haven't memorised it, write the number down on a piece of paper and then erase the number from your phone's memory. Next, place the piece of paper with his number on it in an envelope and seal it shut. On the outside of the envelope, write down all the reasons you don't want to/shouldn't call. It worked for me. Every time I read what I had written, I decided not to call.

whitdb

Write an email instead but do not send it. At least you get it out of your system.

sylviamuchnick

How to know when is the right time to have the conversation about whether he's dating anyone else and let him know that you want to date only him

There is no right time. Remind him frequently that you enjoy his company, but wait till after you've passed a milestone like a birthday or Valentines' day before you bring this up. Notice that I said AFTER the milestone. Guys freak out if you make them have a serious conversation on a holiday.

Masi

How to keep him wanting more of you

Be gloriously happy and fun to be around. Laugh at his jokes. Crack your own. Goof off together. Tell him – sincerely – little ways in which he's absolutely fabulous.

zbandicoot

How to be a woman men love

Things Every Man Loves In A Woman:

You are an independent woman, not a clinger.

You are sexy, hot, but not slutty.

You remember to do the little things, just like you did in the beginning.

You let him pursue you.

You never utter the words, 'Where is this going?'

You impose a two-drink maximum on yourself when you go out.

You never humiliate him in front of friends, family or co-workers.

You watch your language.

You say yes.

textinthecity

Relationships

or

Even my shrink says it's your fault

The best dumping line

'I think I fancy your dad' always seems to work!

curlytops

'I think you're the one. When I think about you all I want to do is plan our wedding and imagine how darling our children will be.' Never fails.

sozo

How to break up if you live together

I just asked my partner what he would do if he made me unhappy. He said he would leave, so I said, 'I'm unhappy.' He left.

sandie

How to get over a marriage break-up

Wake up. Get out of bed. Stay out of bed as much as you can. Clean your home of his belongings, but don't be mean. Box them up nicely, fold everything, etc. Put his stuff somewhere out of the way where you don't have to look at it. Give it time. Do all the things you want to do that you haven't been doing while married. Give it more time. And one day, when you wake up, the hurt won't be there any more.

bookluvinmo

How to fall out of love with him

Make a list of all the things you DON'T like about him (like forgetting your birthday, never calling when he said he would). Read it several times a day, and particularly if you're about to pick up the phone to call him.

manhattanminx

How to get over him

Delete all his texts, all his emails and his number from your phone. Tell all your friends you don't want updates on how he's doing and it will help you get over him quicker.

Makenzie

Remember – 'No man is worth your tears, and the one who is won't make you cry!'

Louie

Be an actress! At first, getting over someone is a decision, not a feeling. The feeling of really being over him comes later, and in the meantime, if you run across him, imagine that you are Meryl Streep playing a part. Act indifferent. Polite, but distracted. Eventually you'll get over him. There are lots more fish in the sea!

asildem

How to stop yourself going back to your ex

Write down as many bad things about your ex as possible. These can range from how badly he treated you to his weird bathroom habits or addiction to sports – but the more, the merrier. Then take another sheet of paper and write down all *your* good qualities. This is a great thing to do with a girlfriend or family member you're really close to. Let them encourage you to identify all those good points you aren't even aware of! Then sit back and compare the two lists. Who looks like the better package for a new relationship, you or him?

Ladypenelope

How to know if you're over him

If his number is still in your phone but, at no point, no matter how drunk or lonely you feel, are you ever tempted to call or text him.

Annabel

How to make a long-distance relationship work

Been there, done that. Make sure you both want the same thing – a steady relationship. Take advantage of as many different methods of communication as you can – cards, letters, email, phone, instant messaging, etc. Get mobile phones from the same network so you can call each other for free, and then use them! Plan your in-person visits for holidays etc whenever possible. Make the visual connection as well: use a webcam to 'date' each other online. It will take creativity and lots of communication, but it can be done.

ImageCoach

My boyfriend and I had 'movie/TV dates' where we would watch the same thing and be on the phone at the same time.

Jrizzony

How to be good in bed

1. Be hungry for it. Show some initiative, and take the lead.
2. Don't wait for him to tell you what to do. Trial and error. Experiment.
3. Make some sound. Show him you're enjoying yourself.
4. Don't scream like a porn star, unless that's what comes naturally.
5. Make sure your sheets are clean.
6. Swallow.
7. Ask him for what you want.
8. Let yourself go. He's not thinking about how fat your thighs are, or how small your boobs may be. He's thanking God he's in this moment.
9. Learn to put a condom on with your mouth.
10. Vary what you're doing.

buddha

Be confident and enthusiastic. No one is always 'good in bed'. Everyone has insecure 'off' days, and partners that it just doesn't go smoothly with, but acting as if you love sex and, more importantly, love your body makes a big difference to how you feel about the sex you are having.

benjizoot

How to get him to talk more

My fella never talks – until I stop talking! Then I think he gets worried and starts asking me questions! Mission accomplished.

Notwop

How to get your husband to get into therapy

Tell your husband you need his help. Don't tell him you think there is anything wrong with him or that he needs therapy or he'll surely dig in his heels. Few people will refuse to help someone in need. Once he's come with you it will be up to the therapist to determine what your husband might need and how to get him to keep coming. Having a male therapist who is older than your husband might help.

sandrasimmons

1. Try to find a man therapist, so he doesn't feel as if you're ganging up on him.
2. Tell him why you think you need this (i.e. need him to be on the same page as you).
3. If he won't go with you, leave the door open. You're going to do this, he's welcome to come.

Midorable

How to forgive him for paying for a lap dance

I'm a lap dancer and can honestly say it is harmless fun. Some men have come in for dances then a few minutes afterwards say they're going home to give their other half a 'good time' . . . My point is that yes, they get turned on by the dancers, but it goes no further than that, and their sexual thoughts return to their partner and what they'll do to them when they get home. Most lap dancers have morals and do the job purely for money. I and the dancers I work with keep things strictly professional and the men respect that too. He may have had a lap dance, but the rules are strict and it's you he goes home to.

missphant

How to get over resentment

Remember what the great Carrie Fisher once said: 'Resentment is like drinking poison and waiting for the other person to die.' Go ahead and be resentful for up to a day, just to indulge this very human feeling. Then make the conscious decision to get over it and move forward. Don't give the other person the power to make you miserable.

CeeVee

How to deal with the fact that your man sits down when having a pee

You should be totally thrilled . . . millions of overbearing women try to train their men to do exactly that so that they don't pee all over the floor and seat! Just don't mention it to any of his friends – but you should definitely see it as a bonus.

Hillary

How to keep the romance alive

Communication is key but can get lost in daily life. Make sure you take time out to reconnect by having a weekly date night. It doesn't need to be expensive or even romantic. Sometimes my Sweetie and I just do the grocery shopping together. Just do something where you can talk to each other with no kids around.

sandrasimmons

How to keep your sex drive active when you're still really interested but just too tired in the evenings etc

Make plans to have sex – make it the best part of your day/week/month, whatever . . . talk about it, think about it, plan what you want to have happen. Sounds kind of weird, but will help you get excited about it. Also, on nights when you don't feel in the mood, let him know, and let him try to find your mood for you. Sometimes, having someone near and caring for you will arouse your sex-drive when you don't expect it to. Women are most often open to sexual intimacy when they feel close to their partner. Males feel close to their partners after having had sexual intimacy. Spending time with your partner, where you are sharing and exploring each other may help bring those feelings to the surface.

ramee151

How to stop your relationship becoming boring and stale

Go out and do things . . . book different things to do that you wouldn't normally, like mini-cruises, day breaks, wall climbing, car racing, anything, and do it spontaneously.

nicolet

How to make yourself his top priority

Be your own top priority. If you do not put yourself first, who will? No one will ever look out for you better than YOU. Be your own worst critic – but also your own best friend. Learn to be self-reliant so that you can survive – THRIVE – on your own, yet be equal in a partnership.

rachbu

How to keep your boyfriend keen

Make sure you are always the first to end telephone conversations.

Cali

How to make him jealous

Send yourself flowers with no card. They become a non-specific threat.

Alessandra

Make sure that when you are walking down the street you maintain eye contact with another man in a flirtatious way without your man seeing so that the man carries on checking you out. Ideally walk a couple of steps ahead when doing this!

leylasadr

How to poop at your boyfriend's house discreetly

1. Always go in after he's been, so he won't be going back too quick.
2. Go before your bath or shower.
3. Matches and air freshener give the game away. You can hear the spray, and both have their own smell. I put the plug in the sink and run the hot water tap on full, then pour some hand soap into the stream – it all steams up and makes the bathroom smell like the soap! Which is how you'd expect it to smell, only stronger (though I doubt anyone will notice).
4. If it's evening, step three works even better with face wash because you use more of it and it usually smells more strongly anyway, plus it's your excuse for being in there longer.

Wow, I have put WAY too much thought into this.

princess83

How to get over your boyfriend's past relationships

You have to remember that whatever happened before you came along, it is YOU that your boyfriend is with now. Do not worry or constantly wonder about what happened before – it will not make anything better or help you and it will just annoy your boyfriend.

Lynz

How to know if you should tell your boyfriend if you accidentally cheated on him

The only real rule in these situations is to treat others how you would wish to be treated yourself. If you do decide to tell him, you should give him as much respect and dignity as you can. (Try not to tell others who will gossip about it and make him feel foolish – he did nothing wrong.)

Wendy

How to know the symptoms of an unfaithful partner

Receiving mysterious phone calls when he only answers in monosyllables ('Mmmm, yes, no, OK').

Arranging to meet up with mates and being coy about telling you where he's going, then not being obtainable while he's out.

Saying he's bought himself clothes (especially around his birthday or Christmas) or other items when he wouldn't normally.

New underwear (my ex actually had a pair of purple silk boxers – big alarm bells).

Making more effort with his appearance.

Visiting his mum more often, doing overtime, going to the gym (Oh Yeah!).

More miles on his car milometer than there should be.

The other woman will do all she can, usually, to help the wife find out, so look out for perfume smells, lipstick marks, greetings cards he's hidden.

Oh! I could write a book . . .

COLIYTYHE

How to cope with a violent partner

No one should ever have to 'cope' with a violent partner. If someone mistreats you, it means that he/she has no respect for you and what is a relationship without respect? The next time that they begin to get violent just leave. Don't try and fight back or try reasoning. When people see red they just see red. When he starts to become aggressive, just try to stay calm and leave the building. Go and stay with friends or family. Wait until the morning to speak to him. Tell him that his behaviour is unacceptable. You deserve better. I'd get out before he gets out of control. Find someone else who will love and respect you and never think of hurting you. Take care of yourself!

sophie08

Get help: you can't do it alone. It's not as simple as just telling him, 'If you can make a fist you can wrap your hand around the doorknob and get out.' If you don't have a network of friends that you can trust to help you (one friend alone can't do it, and some well-meaning people make things worse), surf the net for a support group or therapist who can lead you to a 'safe house'. Get yourself to the point where you decide that if you leave you won't go back. And don't expect your partner to change.

Masi

How to decide if he is the one

He understands.
He tells you.
He shows you.
He listens to you.
He's happy around you.
He compliments you.
He notices when you change something about your appearance.
He takes care of you.
His friends and family like you.
He appreciates you.
He asks for your opinion.

textinthecity

Does he make you laugh and does he laugh at your jokes? A shared sense of humour is very important.
Is he caring and helpful when you are ill?
Is he tolerable when HE is ill?
But if you have to ask those questions, he is possibly NOT the one! You should just know, I think.

operatix

How to get your boyfriend to commit

Consolidate his mind by dumping him . . . if he is the right one, he will come and get you. If he doesn't, you have done the right thing.

Cheekster

Weddings

or

I *am* relaxed

How to buy an engagement ring

When buying an engagement ring with your boyfriend, take him to a
really expensive shop first, then he'll think the next place is a bargain.

Piper

How to make planning a wedding a happy experience (relaxed approach)

Always bear in mind that planning a wedding can be a stressful exercise
and that a wedding really is the most important day of most people's
lives. Make every effort to be patient and tolerant to each other, even if
everyone else seems to be getting tetchy. You will all look back on it with
love and joy.

Cali

How to make planning a wedding a happy experience (organised approach)

Forward Planning: make a draft timetable for the wedding and reception.
Include everything that must happen. Circulate amongst relevant people.
Get a consensus. Finalise timetable. Hire someone who's not personally
involved to keep everyone – including all the staff as well as the bridal
party – on schedule.

catinthehat

How to keep the cost down but still have a glamorous wedding

See if any friends/relatives have a hidden skill e.g. cake making.

Cut out the sit-down meal by having the wedding later in the day. This also cuts out the need for seating plans and place cards. If you are settled in your home together already, you could ask people to bring something there for a buffet, or something to drink, instead of presents.

Try to use flowers that are in season, they will be cheaper and you may be surprised.

Look on the internet for your dress. There is something for everyone out there, for your bridesmaids too. Also, the high street has some great finds.

Don't be afraid to negotiate on prices for the reception, especially if it's during the week.

Candles and balloons make great table decorations and are cheaper than flowers.

flower

How to ensure perfect wedding photos

1. With bright sun, ask the photographer to use the flash. This eliminates those deep, sunken-eyed shadows from faces.

2. Hire a 'photo boss' – someone who's familiar with the 'cast of characters' at your wedding. This person's job is to round people up for each photo so YOU don't have to!

3. Give your photo boss a list of all the photos you really want. If your godmother were to die six months after the wedding, you don't want to then realise with horror that you forgot to have a photo taken with her!

4. Hold your bouquet lower than feels natural. It looks best in photos if you hold it between your mid-thigh and waist.

5. Stand up straight!

CeeVee

How to save money on wedding flowers

Have the florist make arrangements that will be suitable for both the ceremony and the reception. This way they can be moved to the next location. Individual flowers can be cut from church arrangements and reused as decor on the place settings.

Harmony

You can use your bridesmaid's bouquets for centrepieces at the reception. Or use one as a cake topper.

amycov

How to get live classical music at your wedding for a fraction of the cost of professionals

Check with your local university. Most offer music courses. Choose advanced students who want to make extra money by performing at events.

Felicia

How to give young bridesmaids something to do other than throw confetti

Bubbles are a great – and inexpensive – thing to add fun to a wedding, and it gives little bridespeople something to do when you come out of the service. They also look really cool in photos! Rice can be very painful when thrown!

LevantineLass

For one of the weddings I recently participated in, the bride had made 'activity packs' for the child attendants to use during the ceremony and reception. It included things like colouring books and coloured pencils, kids' books, stuffed animals, little games. One of the children made her a wedding card during the ceremony – it's one of her keepsakes now.

ramee151

How to make petal confetti

Don't be seduced into buying expense lavender or rose-petal confetti. Just dry rose petals in a tray in the airing cupboard for a few days and store in a cardboard box till you have enough.

Acantha

How to incorporate your favourite charity into your wedding

Consider adding a request for donations to your favourite charity to your wedding present list.

koily01

How to get people talking at weddings

We made place cards out of homemade party crackers (commonly used at Christmas). The papers we selected looked beautiful, but more importantly, as guests began pop them, the toys inside gave them something to do and discuss. It worked, even at our formal wedding.

burbanovsky

Write a quiz about the bride and groom (yourselves!) before the big day, with a range of questions that different people will be able to answer. On the day, have copies together with pencils on the tables for people to complete when they are seated. Gets everyone talking to everyone to see who knows the answers. You can have a prize for the winning table too!

Notnigella

Parenting

or

I'm beginning to appreciate my mother after all

How to prevent indigestion during pregnancy

Ginger really worked for me, in any format – ginger nut biscuits, extract of ginger (health food shops) etc. Also peppermint creams.

princessbella

I ate a few fennel seeds (about half a teaspoon). It worked great for me, and felt much less medicinal.

mikcers

How to avoid stretch marks

Try breaking open a few capsules of vitamin E and adding it to either cocoa or shea butter. Warm the mixture up in your hands and massage it in wherever you are worried that you'll get stretch marks or cellulite.

Masi

Find the right stretch-mark cream that suits you – bio oil, cocoa butter etc – and get your partner to rub it in every night. It's fun, he's happy to do it (which means it will get done every night without fail or much prompting), and it gets him involved with the pregnancy. It also saves you the hassle of trying to reach over the bump and bend over, and you get a 'bit' of a massage!

Amelia

How to deal with water retention

Mix juniper essential oil with your body oil/moisturiser to get rid of water retention – this is amazing, my ankles halved in size!

Bridget

How to turn over in bed during the last few weeks

Buy a cheap satin chemise nightie and you'll just slide and glide!

Billiedodd

How to breastfeed

Remember which breast you last fed from by moving a bracelet from wrist to wrist. Really easy and really helpful – and a great excuse to buy yourself a pretty new bracelet.

Valerie

How to aid breastfeeding

Breastfeeding seriously dehydrates the mother's body so at least 8 glasses of water a day is a must. Whole milk is also important because breastfeeding saps most of the mother's calcium supply and leaves her open to developing osteoporosis later in her life. The fat is needed because it is a healthy and essential supplement for the baby.

maryzeee

During breastfeeding, drink as much fennel tea as you can to help with milk production.

LadyHelenTaylor

How to use up nipple cream once you've stopped breastfeeding

As a lip-balm! Works brilliantly!

LevantineLass

How to heal stitches fast

Twice a day sit in a bowl of warm water with a few drops of lavender oil and a few of tea tree. This stops infection, heals and is great for soothing when the stitches get really itchy!

perky

How to pee after you've just given birth

Peeing immediately after you've given birth is incredibly painful. As you pee, pour a tooth-mug of warm water between your legs. It really helps.

Marina

This might sound silly . . . but put Vaseline, just a touch of it, on the 'torn' area before you pee. Part of what is so painful is the uric acid getting in the wounds – Vaseline will create a shield.

yaylaliza

How to poo after you have just given birth

Place your feet on two phone directories or something else that will raise them. It eases the pressure and makes the whole experience a little bit more bearable.

ljp67

How to feel great after having a baby

Make half an hour a day for 'you time'. YOU CAN FIND IT! Either do your makeup, read a magazine, paint your nails or whatever makes you feel great. And get dressed first thing in the day. This will motivate you to do something worthwhile with your day instead of sitting in your PJs watching Jeremy Kyle!

vintageprincess

How to keep a post-birth marriage happy

Don't forget the bloke who was there in the first place. Pre-baby you both may have got used to putting him first – it can take a while for him to adjust!

Dorothy

Put baby to bed at seven p.m. every night, starting from the first day you get back from hospital. That way there is one certainty in your day – that at seven p.m. you can sit down and have a glass of wine or a bath, and turn back to your marriage/relationship, even if just briefly! Do this even if the baby is not ready for a sleep – it gives him or her a certainty too and will really help establish a routine.

LevantineLass

Your husband will be the one still around when your child leaves the nest, so it's worth making the investment in having time with him too.

Amelia

How to know when it's 'safe' to have sex again

It's a myth that you can't get pregnant while breastfeeding.

Pamela1958

I have personal experience with sperm that lasted eight days (like the miracle of Hanukkah!), even though everything I've read says no more than seven. So you might want to avoid 'relations' for at least nine days before ovulation. The egg theoretically only survives a day or so after ovulation, so you should be able to resume three or four days after ovulation.

serotonin

How to get a fractious baby to stop crying and sleep

Put the baby down to sleep as usual and turn on the vacuum cleaner. Weird – but it worked for my daughters.

LondonMarian

A tip for babies who are difficult to wind

I'm a nurse in a special care baby unit; a lot of our babies are difficult to wind. This tip can be used by everyone! Place baby on your knee facing away from you (this stops any sick getting on you, though you can do it facing you). Supporting the head and neck and holding the baby firmly, slowly move the baby in circle, without moving the legs. Think of it as if you were sitting on the edge of a bed and you moved the top half of your body in a full circle. It is important to do this gently as you don't want any vomiting! This works because the gentle circular movement encourages the wind to move through the colon. Practise on a teddy bear or doll first to get the idea.

livliv

How to banish the dummy

Santa took our two-and-a-half-year-old's dummy. He took it for children who didn't have one, and left an extra-special present for a kind and generous boy. Santa collected it from under the pillow when he left the presents. It worked MUCH better than expected. We were dreading it. No tears at all!

Clanger

We had 'the dummy fairy' visit us. We told our son what was going to happen a couple of days in advance, just to get him used to the idea that in two more sleeps the dummy fairy would be taking the dummy to give to a baby. On 'the night' he put his dummy into a little basket and put it on the windowsill. In the morning, the dummy fairy left him a present as a thank you. As I recall, he only asked for his dummy twice after that and there were no tears or tantrums! Highly recommend it!

wookiewoo

How to keep wipes moist

I always store mine 'face down'. The liquid that is in the wipes seeps to the bottom wipe, which is really the top wipe and therefore, when you turn the pack the right way up, the top wipe is moist and not dried out.

anassa

How to cure constipation in babies

I find carrot juice a really good cure for constipation, even in babies. Just don't overdo it.

Gretel

Prune juice works wonders really quickly too.

sparkles

Straight apple juice; it doesn't take much, and the babies like the sweet taste.

asildem

How to prevent nappy rash

I use Vaseline on the baby's bum as a barrier to prevent nappy rash. It works well as it's waterproof and is good for the baby's skin. Clean the baby's bottom as usual, then smear on a good amount and pop a nappy on – works wonders for our babies!

livliv

How to ease nappy rash

When changing a nappy, try drying the area thoroughly with a hair dryer on the cool setting, held well away from the skin.

Nigella

How to make a toddler laugh

Admire, and then ask if you can borrow, their clothes. This never fails to elicit a laugh as they tell you raucously that you're FAR too big to borrow them!

CeeVee

How to avoid tantrums

Best advice ever from my mother – NEVER ask a toddler a question to which he can answer NO.

jennyfa

Distract, distract, distract!! If you know the tell-tale signs that a tantrum is coming, then distract your child by playing games such as I-spy etc. Or if you are in the shops, include them, ask them to find the groceries you are looking for, make everything into a game to keep them from getting bored.

LASHES

How to stop tantrums

My grandmother once told me of taking one of my cousins to the shops. My cousin started to throw a tantrum and my grandmother just stopped and said to the people around her, 'Everyone, let's watch Kathryn throw a tantrum!' She said Kathryn quietened down in a hurry, and she never had that problem with her again.

sandrasimmons

With my kids, once a tantrum starts we all leave the room except for the tantrum thrower. I also turn off the telly or any other distraction. Each time the child calls me back into the room, I quietly state that we will talk about it when they are calm. The first few times, it can carry on for ages, but eventually you will only be out of the room for a minute before they are apologising.

icemaiden0504

If I was having a tantrum, my mum would say, 'Don't laugh! Don't laugh!' over and over again. I'd collapse into fits of giggles every time.

MaryPlain

To pull this one off you really have to have no shame. When the child begins to throw the tantrum, simply lie down on the floor next to them and start screaming and crying. I've only ever had to use this one once.

dollymeh

How to entertain your toddlers while you get dressed or do your makeup/hair

Most toddlers love to stack and organise things. When I need some uninterrupted time to myself, I take out my special bag of hair rollers. Like most women, I have curlers of all shapes, colours and sizes that I might not use often, but would never get rid of. I make sure that there are no pins, clips or anything dangerous and I dump them all on the floor! Last time, they spent almost an hour playing with them before they started to annoy me.

maryzeee

How to leave your child happy when you leave for work

I was a nanny for a number of years. The best thing is not to just run out of the house, but to prepare in advance. Make sure in the morning that you and your child can have some special time together. Make sure to always remind him/her that you are leaving: 'Remember, Mummy has to leave for work in ten minutes, but I will be back tonight.' Make it a very simple but a very special routine every morning, like getting up and getting ready, having breakfast, and reading a book together. If he/she knows that you have that time together, it will calm him/her down. Have a similar 'special time' when you get home from work.

Melie

Try getting the babysitter to divert his attention after you have kissed him bye-bye (DVD or colouring book etc). As hard as it is, try not to keep going back to reassure him once you have said bye, as this prolongs his tears and your sadness too.

Joolz

How to keep young children and babies amused on long car trips

Buy your child a copy of *The Highway Code* and ask them to look up the meaning of every sign you pass. This keeps my seven-year-old son happy for hours (and has refreshed my memory too!).

alrscjewcr

Take some chalk and mark each child's first initial on one tyre-wall on the car. Every time you stop for petrol, food, etc, see whose initial is closest to the ground. That person gets a prize. Sometimes we gave $1 as spending money for the trip, sometimes the winner got to sit in their preferred seat, sometimes they got something from the 'goodie bag'.

sandrasimmons

How to amuse small children in restaurants

Play the 'what's missing?' game. Each person takes a turn to remove something from the table whilst everyone else closes their eyes. When the item has been hidden beneath the table, the first person to realise what is missing is the winner. Just be careful that the bill isn't due – the poor waitress wondered why we appeared to be praying at the end of the meal!! Even small kids love this game.

Steph

Play the 'A–Z' game using a topic such as girls' names. For each letter, take it in turns to think of a name until someone can't and has to go to the next letter. At the end, count up the number of passes each person has for when they couldn't think of an answer. Fewest passes wins.

nicolamac99

How to end bickering among siblings

This is one of my all-time favourite solutions. When the kids start bickering, tell them they need to sit and hold hands with each other for ten minutes. Just the THOUGHT of having to hold hands will usually stop the bickering – but if it doesn't, the actual FACT of holding hands does the trick. FYI: Tell them if either of them squeals because the other is holding hands too hard, ten minutes are added to the punishment.

CeeVee

If your children squabble about whose turn it is to take the front seat of the car, or whose turn it is to choose something first, you can solve this by writing each child's initials on a day of the calendar, alternating. Monday is child number one, Tuesday is child number two, Wednesday back to child number one, Thursday is child number two, and so on for every day of the month. On the day that the child's initials are on the calendar, that is her day, and all day long she gets first choice on everything. If there's a disagreement, just say, 'Who's day is it?' This completely solved squabbling for my kids, for years.

asildem

How to curtail nastiness between siblings

If you are at your wits' end with siblings being nasty to each other, tell them that the consequence is going to be the purchasing and wearing of a T-shirt printed with 'I love my (sister or brother) (sibling's name)'. Our son had to buy a shirt and we took it to a shop with an embroidery machine. His shirt said 'I love my sister, Shelby' and he had to wear it on several occasions (to school) much to his chagrin. The mere mention of the shirt has brought him around many times.

sandrasimmons

How to get children to behave

We do a behaviour star chart, and at the end of earning a certain number of stars they may get a treat. Also good is a 'time out' for bad behaviour. They go to a special chair, or sit on the stairs on their own, to think about their behaviour. I will never say, 'You are this, or you are that,' but, 'Your behaviour is this or that.' I believe in a lot of praise for everything; it's good for instilling confidence. The biggest gift we can give our children is confidence and self-esteem. A lot of parents worry about extra maths tutorials, but if you can help them to be happy with themselves you're on the right track.

TaniaBryer

To be sure that children behave in public, be sure to always bring a bag of age-appropriate toys and books. Never expect young children to sit quietly in a public place. Keeping surprises in your handbag is always a winner. At the supermarket make shopping a game. 'Help Mummy find . . .' and ask for an appropriate item, for instance, something green or with the letter L or their favourite cereal. Engage them in the process.

krmrn

How to measure things to share

Sharing of toys by time is easy when you use a kitchen timer which pings! When it's pinged, it's time to pass the toy over.

Clanger

How to get your children to pick up after themselves

We tell our kids they don't need to worry about picking up after themselves, and that we're happy to do it – BUT (and this is a big 'but') they're well aware that if WE pick something up (toys, clothes, shoes) we have the option of giving it away or throwing it out. This generally keeps them in line and picking up after themselves.

CeeVee

When I was young, I had to use my allowance to buy back any toys/clothes/shoes I left lying around. I became tidy *and* thrifty!

CassandraM

How to deal with a bored child

For those long afternoons, have a 'job jar'. Fill it with folded slips of paper, each of which has a chore or activity on it. Have the child draw out a slip, and really follow through with making him do whatever's on it. Have a few fun ones in there, too!

asildem

If they are under ten, get them to lie down on lining wallpaper (very cheap per roll) and you draw round their outline. Give them a box of crayons and tell them to draw themselves – full size.

patsharp

How to help your child deal with a bully

When my daughter was eight, a former friend of hers – we'll call her Brianne – suddenly turned into a bully and gave my daughter no peace. There was nothing physical – just meanness and rudeness. I told my daughter one thing bullies hate is cheerfulness and politeness. We practised her responses to things Brianne would say. This REALLY helped – kind of like studying for a test, I guess. Pretending to be Brianne, I'd say something rude to my daughter and my daughter would respond by being perky and cheerful. Our two favourite and most effective responses to anything Brianne would say were: 'Thanks for letting me know!' and 'Sorry you're feeling so crabby today!' It worked WONDERS and drove Brianne crazy enough that within two or three days, she started avoiding my daughter!

CeeVee

How to teach children about gossip

We tell our kids that if they feel the urge to gossip, they just need to ask themselves two simple questions:

1. Is it kind?
2. Is it true?

If they can't say 'yes' to both questions, then they probably don't need to share whatever it is they want to say about another person. We also tell them that they should picture someone saying the same thing about them – and ask how it would make them feel.

CeeVee

How to help children get through the fear of getting injections

You may laugh at this one but it worked for me! Starting when my children were small enough to understand that injections can sting, I would tell them to hold on tight to my hand and I would let my bravery flow out of me and into them. It worked every time with all three of my children (two girls and a boy – now eighteen, seventeen and fifteen).

sandrasimmons

How to get a nine-year-old to swallow a tablet without gagging

Two ideas:

1. Have her swallow it with something thick like yoghurt, so she can't feel it as it goes down her throat.
2. Practise with Tic-Tacs.

blueberrymuffin7

How to avoid sugary cereals

Both my children love Weetabix, porridge and healthy cereals, but when supermarket shopping they will ask for the sugary, fancy-packaged, free-toy types (of course!). For a treat I will sometimes buy what they want, but to avoid giving them a bowlful, they have their normal cereal with just a sprinkling of the sugary/chocolaty one on top. They feel as if they've had a big treat, and I'm happy because I know they've had their complex carbohydrate!

blueskye

How to get children to eat vegetables

Try growing your own veggies; even with a small garden or patio you could put tomatoes or potatoes into pots, even carrots. We have a small patch of garden and have beans, carrots and potatoes growing. Kids love to see the process of planting, watering and harvesting, and the food tastes so much better.

COLIYTYHE

I feed my kids raw veggies as snack food while they watch TV. They are so engrossed in watching, they will eat anything fed to them, especially if it's just before supper and they are getting hungry.

woozle

How to get your children to eat fruit

If you freeze a banana, you can tell them it's an ice lolly.

Sadie

If you freeze grapes they become like delicious tiny ice lollies! Children adore them and grown-ups think they are pretty good too! Plus you do not get any left-over slimy grapes when they become overripe or bruised.

rosepink

How to get a child to eat

If he or she refuses to eat, don't make too much of a fuss: just take their plate away and don't give them anything else to eat until the next mealtime – no matter how much they whine.

Dacia

How to brush sand off wet kids painlessly

Sprinkle on lots of cheap talc – the sand drops off and dressing is easy peasy.

Clanger

How to clean up after a children's painting session

If you put a little Fairy Liquid into children's paints before they start, it makes it a lot easier to clean up. It doesn't affect the paint at all.

Rosa

How to keep track of all those tiny bits and pieces of games

Sellotape a resealable freezer bag to the inside lid of the games box and keep all the little bits in there.

Willa

How to instil a love of museums

Don't try and go around a whole museum in one day. Sensory overload will kick in, and you'll end up enjoying none of it. First buy a guidebook. Then – over a coffee elsewhere – decide on one room/exhibition/single exhibit to visit. Go straight to that area/piece, enjoy it, and leave. Repeat this another day, or even a few hours later, to see other pieces.

pgrier

How to not lose a child whilst out

Write your mobile number on the inside of their shirt/coat, and ask them to tell an adult in uniform or an adult with a family to phone you.

Gwiddon

We always tell our young son (six) that if he gets separated from us while out to look for someone in a uniform (even in a shop, staff often can be identified) or a lady who looks like a granny. We have taught him our address and home phone number, and he will sometimes wear a wristband with our mobile phone numbers on. We have told him that if someone tries to take him away he should shout, 'No, No, No! You're not my mum!' and make a fuss if he can, to draw attention to himself.

COLIYTYHE

How to be prepared for kids being sick in the car

I keep a couple of empty ice-cream or washing capsule tubs in my car – you know, the plastic tubs with lids on. If my young 'un is going to be sick, at least he can aim it into the tub. You then put the lid on and put it in a bin next time you stop, either at home or en route. Make sure you get the next one ready after though! Keep some Dettol or other strong-smelling disinfectant in the boot too, along with some wipes, to mop up any spills and to mask the smell!

COLIYTYHE

How to help your kids read faster

Get your kids to watch foreign films on TV – more specifically, ones with subtitles. Your child will want to keep up with the subtitles and plot, so he will be forced to learn to read faster or fall behind. That speed-reading will transfer from television to books. The film can be educational or not. Japanese animated films called *anime* are great – they're fun and amusing, but make sure the *anime* is appropriate for your child. Some *anime* are quite mature and graphic.

hummer

How to get rid of head lice

When rinsing my son's hair after it has been shampooed, I put a couple of drops of tea tree oil in the rinsing water. He covers his eyes with swimming goggles(!). Although there have been a few instances of head lice in his school, so far, thankfully, he has remained clear.

COLIYTYHE

Well, first you should know that you should steam clean all beds, sofas, chairs etc. Anywhere it is possible for the head to touch. You should get cotton and paraffin, dab the cotton in the paraffin and dab it on the roots of the hair while separating the hair into thin layers. Leave it in for a day, and rinse the next day. It will leave the hair a bit oily, but it kills anything living in there.

Nats

We went through recurring infestations of head lice. Our solution was a disciplined, time-consuming routine of cleaning and checking. First, you must understand the life-cycle of head lice (do a little internet research). Next, everyone in the family must be treated with the lice product and then checked thoroughly and daily to remove all nits (eggs) which are glued on to the hair near the scalp. The lice products may kill the live ones, but they do nothing to get rid of the eggs, which hatch within days and start the cycle again. At the same time, you must understand that lice and eggs can live on cushions/hats/couches etc for a while before dying, and they can restart the cycle on someone else. If we were to get lice now, I would be able to rid us of it completely within two weeks with discipline and patience. Good luck!

amlush

How to get reluctant children to enjoy bath time

When the small one refuses the freshly drawn warm bath, pick him up while cooing words of endearment and carry him gently to the bathroom. Then bung him in the tub, clothes and all. Problem is, after that my son nagged me for years to do it again!

ladydigger

How to get your teenager to communicate

Go for a ride in a car, just the two of you. If you are sitting shoulder to shoulder and you are not making eye contact, it's very easy for the kids to open up. Also, talk to him like an adult. Don't be judgmental. I work with teenagers and I get them to spill their guts fast, because they know that I'll listen without judging. Also, tell them about things you did when you were younger – and not just the goody-two-shoes stuff, but the things that were fun at the time but turned out to be a bad idea. And don't lie about things like drugs. Just tell them it was a different time and you didn't have all the information you needed to make the best choice. Teenagers respect honesty and vulnerability.

Masi

If the teenager is a boy, feed him. If the teenager is a girl, take her shopping. No matter the sex of your teenager, make sure you have dinner together as a family as often as possible. Cooking, eating and cleaning up together naturally makes the perfect climate for conversation.

sandrasimmons

How to deal with saying no to teenagers

Explain why you are saying no and ask them to come up with a solution to every point. Also, if they are going out, a genius move is to allow them to stipulate a coming-home time – I found it was often earlier than the one I would have set.

ladykingston

How to not freak out if you're a first-time mum

Only take what other mothers say with a pinch of salt. Bear in mind that many mothers lie to each other outright, and that mothers of other generations simply do not remember things correctly. So when your mother tells you that you were potty-trained at eight months, smile and thank her, and never give it another thought.

LevantineLass

The best advice I was given was from my mum – telling myself that 'Everything's a phase' has got me through some dark moments as I try to bring up my twins!

sparkles

My advice would be to just go with it. Remember that babies are supposed to cry, supposed to puke all over you, and you're supposed to be completely exhausted most of the time. Make sure you get some fresh air every day – this is especially important in the beginning when the days and nights roll into one! Oh, make sure you can meet up with your girlfriends regularly, to keep yourself in touch with the real world!

ellenback

How to stop arguing with your mother over silly things and get her to treat you more as a friend than an annoying daughter

If the things you argue over are silly, then try not opposing her. While you are letting your mother win silly arguments, go about living your life with dignity and maturity. If the arguments are about things which are more serious, then make a point of showing her that you are considering her opinion. She does, after all, have a lifetime of experience. Acknowledge that, even if you choose not to follow her advice.

asildem

Treat your mum like you would treat one of your friends. When she comes in, offer to make her a drink. If she is struggling with something, offer to help. As she appreciates this she will mellow towards you. Treat her like you would want to be treated and you'll find it should work. It's all about respect and tolerance, not for your elders and betters and parents and children but for another human being, and you will get the same for yourself. Of course I'm a mother answering this one. I have a twenty-two-year-old daughter; yes, she drives me mad sometimes, but guess what – I do the same to her.

sheepish239

This isn't a tip, but my daughter and I used to drive each other crazy most of the time. She died, suddenly, when she was in her twenties, and now I can never forgive myself for not being more loving and less bad-tempered with her, however maddening she might have been. So remember, life can be short, so you should try to keep the peace at all times.

operatix

How to be a popular godparent

If you have lots of godchildren, send them a present on your own birthday instead of theirs – that way you don't have lots to remember. They will get so many presents on their actual birthday, but yours will stand out at another time of year!

LevantineLass

How to strengthen the bond you have with your husband and kids

Once or twice a year, have a family retreat. This means: go grocery shopping at the beginning of the weekend so you're well-stocked for food, then turn off the computer, don't leave the house, don't answer the phone, and spend the whole weekend together, JUST FAMILY. Play board games, play cards, watch movies, and simply spend time together with no distractions. Kids LOVE this, and it's really a wonderful way to pass a weekend.

CeeVee

How to help your children make friends at school

Make an effort to get to know the other parents and try to set up outings or get-togethers that will include the maximum number of kids. The more parties and activities that you organise, the more chances your children have to make friends. Try something like a pizza/video party (non birthday) with a theme, like a fifties' theme to watch *Grease*, or a dinosaur theme for *Night at the Museum*. Have an ice-cream party to watch *Happy Feet* during the summer, and get everyone to try the tap dance at the end of the DVD. Activities must appeal to the masses, so that all the kids want to come. Don't forget to invite both the cool kids and the outcasts if possible.

Masi

How to stop feeling guilty

You cannot be the best mum, best employee, best wife and best woman. Not all together! Don't push yourself too hard. Start being honest with yourself, pointing out what is making you feel guilty. Then, write down what can be achieved and when. If something is not possible for this year, relax. That's life and many women are facing the same challenge.

rafaelpay

For Oldies
or
What was I going to say?

How to improve your memory and conversation

Read something interesting (something as small as a news article, or an internet blog, or even a solution you read here) and share it with a friend. Not only will you have read, but you'll probably have a great conversation, too.

stelladore

How to jog your memory

If you can't remember why you crossed the room or went upstairs, retrace your steps exactly. The action might trigger your memory – if not, don't fret about it. Do something else!

Cali

Tie a knot in your handkerchief. Then don't forget where you've put it.

catinthehat

If I wake during the night and remember something important, I turn the clock away from the bed. In the morning I wonder why I've done that and usually remember! Or throw a pillow on the floor. Anything out of position will jog your memory in the morning.

patsharp

How to flatter your skin

Always wear a flattering pale colour next to your face: pearls, a pale scarf, a white or cream shirt or blouse. Older skin can't cope with dark colours. Sad but true.

Cali

How to prevent wrinkles

Always wear face cream/sunscreen. If you find yourself frowning, stop! You don't have to frown to concentrate. Wear sun specs whether it is winter or summer.

katrina9758

How to age well

You age well by living well. This means taking care of yourself, but more importantly being happy, learning from your mistakes and not making a big deal out of them. There is nothing that looks better on an 'ageing' woman than happiness and a savoir faire that is only attained by living. Living is messy and full of mistakes. Living well means that we deal with these messy problems with grace and this also shows in your face. Make no mistake, sunscreens, moisturisers, water, diet and exercise are important. However, none of this will make an 'ageing' woman more appealing than having lived a full life and come out the other side happy!

byronspsbatt

Moisturise, moisturise, moisturise – and remember that your face doesn't end at the line on your chin where it slopes to become your neck. The décolletage is also a very important area to moisturise as it becomes prominently aged in women's advanced years, specifically because of lack of moisture. I also find that the hands betray a woman's age, no matter how much aid her face has actually had, surgically or not!

VerucaS

Remember: Even when you have a pain, you don't have to be one!

Hetti

How to age happily

Life should not be a journey to the grave with the intention of arriving safely in an attractive and well-preserved body, but rather skid in sideways, chocolate in hand, totally worn out and screaming 'WOO-HOO what a ride!'

clinic2316

How to keep up to date

To stay current, subscribe to a fashion email newsletter, an entertainment news email and check a news website every day.

Masi

How to reduce muscle cramp in the night

To avoid attacks of muscle cramp, drink one tumbler of proper tonic water (not low calorie) per day. This should give your system enough quinine to do the trick.

Cali

The little vertical indentation under your nose is called your fulcrum. Pinch it really hard between your fingers. No idea why it works – do we care?

patsharp

How to face daylight in public

Get an at least 6 × magnifying glass (10 × is better) and look at yourself in a bright light once a month. It's horrible, but better you see than the rest of the world.

Dawn

How to keep up polite conversation with an oldie

Remember it may cause embarrassment to ask an older person what he or she was about to say!

Cali

To become an oldie the person has experienced many things; ask pertinent questions and speak slowly.

clinic2316

How to look good in later years

An older woman always looks good when groomed, and wearing good quality (the best you can afford) clothing that is stylish, simple and well tailored. A well-cut blazer-style jacket, with slacks or skirt, can then be made modern and younger with T-shirts, blouses and ONE new fashion item. This may be a belt in a bright colour or modern-style shoes and bag. Or team the blazer with a good pair of jeans. This will stop you from looking 'like a Nana', and be comfortable at the same time. Also, tone down your makeup if you have always worn it, or start wearing a little if you haven't . . . you will need subtle colouring around your face, to stop you looking washed out and pale.

baby17

How to change your makeup approach as you get older

Generally speaking, the lighter the better – both in terms of the amount you're applying and the colours themselves. Lighter, softer colours will be more flattering and have the added benefit of making your eyes appear brighter and your lips appear fuller. Put the tiniest touch of white (eye pencil is good) at the 'cupid's bow' of your upper lip and at the inner corner of your eyes and both will look better instantly.

CeeVee

How to keep your mind sharp

1. Take up bridge.
2. Swivel your eyes from side to side for thirty seconds each day!!
3. Do Sudoku.

Cali

How to grow old gracefully

Grow old disgracefully – it's more fun.

BamBam

At Work

or

... and you thought school was a minefield

How to stop your boss (or anyone) from making passes at you

As he leers towards you, scrunch up your face, peer closely and say, in a slightly repulsed way, 'You've got something in your teeth' as if it's something really revolting. He should be embarrassed and slink away to remove it . . .

Labink

Make friends with his wife/partner/daughter/son.

leggbarbara

How to manage your boss

'Communicating up' helps. Always keep your boss informed (briefly!) about what's going on with your work. Don't assume she/he already knows this. Asking for regular reviews and welcoming feedback is another good idea. It engages your boss, makes them feel as if you want to succeed/improve, and keeps things from sneaking up on you (i.e. a problem that your boss sees and you have no idea bothers her/him).

bonviv89

Bring an agenda to every meeting – that way you can work through what you need, and not forget anything. Flatter and give them the credit without being a creep. If you make them look good, they'll like you.

Trula

How to stop procrastinating

You only need to know three words to succeed: Don't Dabble – FOCUS!

Melody

If you have one big task which you're finding hard to tackle, try to break it up into manageable chunks. Either commit to finishing a chunk at a time, or to spending a full hour working on the project – with no distractions. Amazing how much I find I can get done in an hour if I stop faffing around and checking my emails every five minutes.

Alice

How to deal with a difficult, older, insecure female boss

Compliment her clothes, accessories etc. Get her talking about herself more. Make her feel really interesting and as if you are looking up to her – in awe almost! Ask her for advice about things that you may already know the answer to, which will make her feel superior and in control. It may be difficult initially, but she will begin to trust in you and you may end up enjoying her company!

whiskas

How to look cool in meetings

If you want to give an impression of seriousness and influence, lean in to the table. Putting your arms on the table (folded in front of you) also adds to that impression. However, if you are in a meeting with people who are trying to sell you something, lean back in your chair to give an impression of casualness – it helps in your negotiations.

A few things NOT to do:

1. Smile too often (though cool smiles are useful, moderate your natural instinct to oversmile).
2. Cross and uncross your legs (gives an impression of nervousness and draws attention to your legs – save it for the hot date!).
3. Play with your hair.
4. Sit with your hands in your lap (hidden hands imply hidden plans – and it makes you look meek).

citygrrl

How to stay calm for a big presentation

Making a speech or big presentation can be scary, but embrace the adrenaline as a super-power that will help you reach great heights. Keep repeating to yourself the mantra: 'I'm not frightened, I'm excited.' It will help you re-frame it as an enjoyable experience – and people who are having fun are much more inspiring and appealing. Whatever you do, don't start with 'I'm so scared/nervous.' No one came to hear you say that – they don't care, and it will make you look inept.

Queenie

How to stop going red when giving a presentation

If you're prone to severe blushing when you give a presentation, write your notes on green paper, or use a green marker on white paper. It's the same premise as colour correction foundation – green neutralises the red.

suejak

How to build a rapport

Actually listen to what the other person is saying rather than focusing on your reaction to it.

Zoe

I agree, everyone loves a good listener. But to build a rapport you need to build trust. Just being honest and not trying to impress someone (relax, you'll impress them with your dazzling personality sooner or later) will lay the foundation for a strong business relationship or friendship. Try not to be too nosey, and offer a little bit about yourself. Someone who wants to know all about you and never reveals anything about themselves could be a manipulator.

Masi

How to be more assertive when job-hunting or freelancing

If you are a freelancer or looking for a job, have some business cards printed with your name, number and email address, even if you don't have a job or job title. Hand them out as much as you can – it will make you feel more confident and people won't lose them as easily as a scrap of paper. Make sure it's a good-quality business card though, not one printed in the Tube.

LevantineLass

How to dress for an interview

Forget about wearing perfume. You may love it but your future employer may not. Wear your makeup naturally. A smart ponytail keeps long hair neat and is still professional. And under almost all circumstances, a suit is a must.

freemoniski

How to do well in a job interview

Research, research, research. If you're serious about the job, you should take the time and show interest in the company. And try to find out as much as you can about the person interviewing you.

Greer

Dress in comfortable clothes (a touch of red is good for confidence); don't try to use words you're not familiar with, in order to impress; don't change your speaking style; know your audience, know your subject, be yourself – and visualise ending to rapturous applause. If you can't believe in yourself, why would anyone else?!

Nursey

Don't wear jewellery – you'll start fiddling with it (trust me you will, even if you don't realise it) and the potential employer will get the impression you are nervous. Also, when you first walk into the room, take a (subtle) sweeping glance round the room. That way you'll not feel inclined to stare at any objects and seem like a freak. It seems obvious, but if you arrive ten minutes early the employer will assume you are more likely to be early than late. Arrive more than ten minutes early and you may seem desperate (and you'll have been seated in reception being bored, so when you go in for 'the kill' you'll have a bored expression on your face, won't be as fresh as you first were, and will probably have an annoying song stuck in your head!). DRESS WHERE YOU WANT TO BE AND NOT WHERE YOU ARE!!

mademoisellepamela

How to follow up after an interview

Don't leave the interview without a timetable of when a decision will be made. Specifically ask if all candidates will be notified, or just those moving to the next step. Specifically ask how notification will be made, via phone or letter. Send a proper note of thanks and follow that up with a phone call if you do not hear.

Whitlo

How to succeed in business

Never wound unless you can kill. It sounds brutal, but if you hurt someone badly, they'll remember. So don't wound unless you can completely take them out.

Callista

How to make more tips

When taking an order try to be at the eye level of the customer. I worked in a fairly casual restaurant, so I would just squat down when taking an order. Also try and personalise the service whenever possible like writing, 'Thank you' and your name on the bill. I did find the eye level thing really seemed to work and increase my tips.

Lilacs

How to be organised

Lists. Lists really are the best way to get yourself organised. Write a list including the most minor of tasks that you need to do; the satisfaction you get from ticking one off will motivate you to carry on with the rest. I am always writing loads of lists for work and, believe me, they really are worth doing because everything won't be going round in your head, it will all be on paper.

LilacSprinkles

At work I find the best way to keep myself organised is to clear my desk before I begin another task. That way I won't get papers confused and I also have a larger space to work on. It makes a hell of a difference as you won't feel as bogged down. Clear desk . . . clear head!

sophie08

How to get people to do what you want

Don't be dictatorial; use language like 'Let's . . .' or 'Shall we try . . .'

Candace

How to regain control of your time from email, etc

Pick just a single time each day when you have X amount of time free – say, thirty minutes or an hour, whatever works for you. Then use this time period and ONLY this time period to check your email and return phone messages. You'll find that it makes you more focused and more attuned to your own personal priorities. Using this approach also takes far less time than checking both regularly throughout the day.

CeeVee

How to deal with a colleague who ignores you

This person could be threatened by you. This is usually why someone is extremely rude or ignores a co-worker, unless they have a defective personality. Take comfort in the fact that you have something that your ill-mannered co-worker wants, e.g., approval of a higher-up, knowledge, wardrobe, good looks, etc. The only way to handle a person such as this is to kill them with kindness, especially when your superiors are nearby. It is so much fun to make the other squirm when they have to be nice!

byronspsbatt

How to get a pay rise or promotion

Almost the most important thing is timing. Don't do it when it suits you, do it when it suits your boss. Learn to read her moods. Don't ask when she is frantically busy or in trouble herself. The best time is when things are going well and she is feeling happy and confident about the future of the company.

Paula

When negotiating a salary, pay rise or promotion, imagine you are doing it on someone else's behalf. It's amazing how coy even the most accomplished women get when asking for money.

Felicia

How to clean your computer

To clean the hardware of your computer (monitor, keyboard, mouse etc) first make sure everything is disconnected from the mains, then, using a microfibre cloth dampened with a white vinegar/water solution and squeezed out well, wipe over. For grimy keyboard keys, a cotton bud moistened with the same mixture, then squeezed out into the microfibre to avoid drips, will get the job done. Do not fear that the vinegar smell will prevail, as it is gone within seconds and takes nasty smells, like cigarettes, with it.

PoshPaws

How to deal with an annoying co-worker

Keep focused on the fact that if you find him or her annoying, it's highly likely that many others do too. Keep evidence of your annoyance very subtle – with a slight frown – while being overly patient and kind. And look out for how many times you catch a sympathetic eye across the room.

Meredith

Understand that wherever you go in life, and whatever you do, you will be confronted with those who seem to be in this world only to make your life more difficult. The high road is more scenic but overrated. Stealing all of the annoying co-worker's staples, paper clips or pens, or 'rearranging' things in their office space, can be a harmless way to make their annoying conduct more bearable.

citytimes

Make them uncomfortable in harmless ways. Sit in your office with the lights off and stare at them, or ask them to attend a cult meeting with you.

citytimes

Travel

or
It'll be worth it when we get there

How to pack

Roll your clothes instead of folding – it reduces the amount of space taken up and prevents creases.

tibbytoos

Roll up a whole outfit together. Then you can just pull out a roll of clothes each day and you won't have to search through the suitcase – rummaging can wrinkle clothes.

stelladore

When you have a very quick trip where you will have to put a dress or suit on immediately for a meeting, fold it around bubble wrap – the air in the wrap, unlike tissue, moves with the garment, so it doesn't crease.

JoMalone

Store the cloth bags that new shoes come in in your suitcase ready to aid fast packing. When the time comes I stuff them with underwear, bikinis, socks and vests. It makes for fast, organised unpacking on arrival too . . . and they double up inside beach bags to protect ipods, cameras etc, or to take dirty laundry home in.

LauraBailey

How to pack shoes

Pack most of your socks inside shoes, and your shoes inside socks.

Johanna

How to travel light and save time packing

Cosmetics are always the heaviest thing in my luggage. I've invested in lots of miniature bottles (you can get them from many chemists) and transferred some of each of my beauty products into these, and keep them in a makeup bag in my cupboard. Whenever I go away, I just grab the bag. It saves time packing up all my cosmetics too!

lubilu

For cosmetics, perfume and skin care, ask for samples each time you purchase (and make friends with the counter girls so that they will provide some before vacation, even if you're not purchasing). Keep the mini-size products in the cosmetic bag in your suitcase so you are always ready to go!

DezG

How to protect against spills while travelling

Always travel with Ziploc bags. I pack everything inside them when travelling. You'll know why if you have ever had an accident with makeup or exploding shampoo. (You can also use them to make a body scrub with honey, salt and lime oil.)

JoMalone

How to pack for two weeks in the sun

Discuss what's needed with your friends. If there are four of you going, you don't all need to take a hairdryer, straighteners, toothpaste, shampoo, conditioner and body washes. Just work out who can take what. If you are the same size in clothes or shoes, see what the others are taking. You can double what you have to wear – but just make sure you decide that, if you both want to wear something, the owner has first dibs.

mojo

How to close a full suitcase

Can't zip up an over-full suitcase? Pile everything in as normal and leave it overnight. It magically seems to sink.

Olwen

How to know which queue to choose when there's more than one

Always choose the queue to the left. Apparently, most people's natural tendency is to go to the right.

sandrasimmons

How to escape a plane crash

Make a note of how many seats there are between your seat and the emergency exit in front of (and behind) you. If the worst happens, it may be dark/smoky, so this way you can 'count' your way to the nearest exit.

monkeyface

How to make a long flight bearable with and for a three year old who doesn't like watching films

It's all about the hype. Tell them that, because they have been so good, you've got a special treat for them to play with on the plane. That way they'll be really excited and just tuck straight into all the little games etc. When I used to baby-sit for the day I'd go on to the internet the night before and print off loads of different colouring-in pages and small easy puzzles, staple it all together and then make a glitzy customised front cover. Went down a storm and it was free! Do the same sort of thing for the journey.

sophie08

How to not get freaked by lost luggage

If you are travelling with someone else, put half your stuff in their case and half of theirs in yours – if one case does go missing, then you will have some stuff with you until the missing one turns up. Don't put anything with your full home address on the outside of the case though.

COLIYTYHE

How to cope with lost luggage

Don't forget to make a list of all the items packed – you can even photograph them if they are laid out on your bed. Very helpful for insurance claims! Also, have an accurate description of your suitcase dimensions, make and colour.

stephh

How to ensure that losing your passport doesn't ruin your holiday

When travelling, keep a paper copy of your passport – if you lose your passport or if it's stolen, the copy will assist you to get a replacement or new passport quickly.

Midge

Scan your passport and email it to yourself. If anything happens to it, just open your email and print off a copy.

IrishGirl

How to guard your handbag in a public loo

Wash your hands in the basin nearest the blow dryer, or equip yourself with paper towels before washing, so that your handbag isn't left unguarded while you dry your hands.

Cali

How to get the wrinkles and creases out of your clothes

If you arrive at a hotel to find your shirts or dresses wrinkled, hang them in the bathroom whilst you shower. Be sure to close the door and get the bathroom quite warm, damp and steamy . . . the wrinkles disappear.

Melody

How to cope with a hotel fire

Always check the fire exit when you arrive, and always have a torch in your room. You might have to run down a pitch-dark staircase.

Melody

How to be identified in an emergency

Make sure you have two contact numbers stored under the name 'ICE' (In Case of Emergency) in your mobile phone.

Flavia

How to deter hotel thieves

If your hotel's security could be better, then always leave the Do Not Disturb sign hanging on your door.

Samantha

How to remove tar picked up at the beach from your feet

My granny always used butter. It works!

leggbarbara

Nail polish remover works really well. Also, baby oil or lighter fluid, believe it or not!

jsa

How to make the most of a city

Ask a few people – from a local taxi driver to a fruit seller to a hotel employee – what the best restaurant in the city is. Ask them where they would go to celebrate, rather than recommending a place for tourists.

LevantineLass

How to keep the mozzies away

Use tea tree oil. It's quite an earthy smell and you do get used to it, but insects hate it, particularly the mosquitoes. A few dabs on vulnerable areas does the trick. I also rub it around window and door frames during summer. The aroma that the insects can detect keeps them away.

carolec

Take vitamin B supplements. It works a treat.

Hobbit

How to stop luggage smelling musty

Keep old slivers of scented soap in the pockets.

Bianca

A couple of drops of essential oil on a tissue in the pockets will keep luggage smelling sweet and also prevent bacteria and other nasties.

meeze

Put a dryer sheet inside. This keeps the luggage from smelling musty while it's not being used. A fresh dryer sheet included while packing for a trip will ensure your clothes don't end up with that 'cargo hold' smell upon arrival.

dabasan

Christmas

or

Christmas comes but once a year . . . it just feels like twice

When to make Christmas pudding and mince pies

Always make the mincemeat for mince pies in September, but make your Christmas pudding a whole year in advance. It really does make a difference.

Zenobia

How to prepare for Christmas

Make a list OF Christmas, not just a Christmas list: the menu, the food shopping, food preparation, where and what decorations. Christmas comes every year!

India

How to stop pine needles dropping from a Christmas tree

Add a tablespoon of honey to the water that you use for the tree. This mimics the sap of the tree and ensures that the needles don't drop so much.

pgrier

How to create heirloom ornaments

Have simple silver ornaments engraved with the names of immediate family members, grandparents, and pets. When someone passes away, their ornament is hung at the top of the tree, 'close to heaven'. When a new pet arrives, or a baby is born, have a new ornament engraved. When children go off on their own, they take their ornament with them to hang on their own first tree. Every year it is meaningful when my children hang Grandma's ornament 'up near heaven'.

asildem

How to prevent yourself from going broke at Christmas

Two words: Secret Santa: when the members of a group pick just one name out of a hat and buy a gift for that person. Rather than trying to cover every one of your friends and going broke in the process, organising Secret Santas with different groups of your friends can ease the present-giving process, leaving you more time and money to produce just one thoughtful gift.

hummer

How to wrap presents for young children

Use the coloured funnies section from the Sunday paper.

vampriss666

If you have more then one child, try to use different paper for each one. That way it's easy to distinguish which present is whose when they're all stacked under the tree.

sophie08

How to decorate on the cheap

Got spare fairy lights? Get out your vases and fill them with the lights. Arrange the vases on top of a surface where you can plug in the lights without the cord going across the floor, such as on top of the TV cabinet.

Jillaroo95

How to enhance placements etc at Christmas

Decide on the colour theme you want for your Christmas table that corresponds with your decor and tree; then choose shiny good-quality Christmas wrapping paper and wrap it round your placemats, coasters etc. Your table will look colourful and Christmassy!

gillybags1

How to decorate the table

Forget a fancy flower centrepiece (they don't last in centrally heated rooms). Just pile clementines (with leaves attached preferably), fir cones and shiny baubles on a dish or plate.

waynetta

Wired ribbons cut into the appropriate length and fastened with a drop of glue make wonderful festive napkin rings.

Ilana

How to make brandy butter look more appealing

A light sprinkling of nutmeg on top of brandy butter makes it look pretty.

Felicia

How to stop overeating at Christmas

To stop yourself overeating at Christmas simply tie a piece of string around your waist before the meal – under your clothes. It shouldn't be too tight, you should be able to get a fist between it and you. When it starts to draw blood you should probably stop eating!

Minerva

What to do with old Christmas cards

Cut round the pretty bit of a card (pinking shears are ideal) either in a square, round or oblong shape. Punch a hole at the top, thread with pretty ribbon and use as parcel labels. Ensure there's no writing on the other side!

waynetta

When my children were small, I used to cut up the cards into various
shapes, depending on their age, and turned them into jigsaw puzzles.

pippinpuss

How to store Christmas-tree lights

Roll up a thick newspaper and Sellotape it into a tube then wind the
lights around it. To decorate next time, simply unwind and there are no
tangles. Otherwise, use a cardboard tube container.

Judi

How to store delicate decorations

If you have one of those drawer tidies that has divisions for your socks, it
will work just as well in a cardboard box to keep your baubles separated
and safe. Also, those polystyrene apple trays work just as well.

Theresa

Present Giving

or

I can't buy you love, long life or happiness . . .
so will a handbag tide you over?

How to bring a great houseguest present

Instead of flowers or chocolate, take a bundle of new good books when you go to stay with someone. A selection of the latest bestsellers is always welcome. Also, a selection of hard-to-find magazines, especially if you are going to the countryside, makes a good present – e.g. *The New Yorker*, *National Geographic* etc.

LevantineLass

What about a magazine subscription sent with your thank you letter. One appropriate for their hobby would be nice. *The English Garden* is a lovely one for gardeners and not easy to find in shops.

patsharp

What to do when your gift to the hostess is returned by her when she visits you

Give it back to her the next time you visit, and see how many times the gift goes back and forth before you both admit you'd have preferred a bottle of gin.

pgrier

How to give for a special occasion

To make a milestone birthday (like a thirtieth or fortieth) even more memorable, plan ahead and buy thirty (or whatever number) small gifts, wrap each individually, and give one per day for each of the thirty (forty, fifty) days leading up to that birthday. Soap, candy, inexpensive earrings, etc are great ideas, and the recipient gets to celebrate in advance of the big day. Smiles all around!

Inmop

How to create the perfect gift for very close friends

For a perfect gift for a momentous occasion, simply buy a photo album with adhesive pages. Then on the double-page spreads, place pictures of other friends on the left pages, and on the opposite pages have them write personal messages. In the rest of the book just place other cool pics! After placing photos and messages, decorate to finish. It's great if you have a group of close friends. It's a perfect gift for 18th birthdays. I did one for my close friend and she said it was her favourite present!

seksykt

How to give the perfect wedding gift

Follow their wedding list. Believe me . . . you may think the knives and forks are a really dull present to buy, but they are usually really wanted. It is frustrating to get half the cutlery set from one person and find that other friends have gone off piste and bought you a fluorescent green vase instead!!

loop118

It's amazing how many couples look back on their special day and wish they had more pictures. Give the newlyweds a customised gift that they'll cherish forever: take pictures at their wedding and create a coffee-table book with all the candid shots.

AdvocateForSmiles

How to be prepared

Buy birthday, Christmas, engagement and baby cards as you see them, so you're ready for every occasion.

Alice

How to buy the perfect gift

If you're unsure of what to get, fill a large gift bag with lots of small gifts that you know will come in handy and prevent the person having to purchase items they normally use (for instance, magazines, a certain face wash, lip gloss, etc. Just think how much you'd love it!).

Kirsten

How to send great flowers

Request that the arrangement be composed of a single type of flower, in a uniform colour. This prevents ragged, cheap-looking arrangements from a remote florist. Even an arrangement of all daisies or carnations looks better than a similarly priced 'spring bouquet', which is florist code for leftover alstroemeria and fern leaves shoved into a basket.

fashionvictim

How to tie a bow that does not go crooked/lopsided

When you're tying the actual bow bit, take your ribbon or whatever over first, rather than under, and your bow will be straight.

thepoet

Pets

or

The closest thing to being a parent,
without the hassle of finding a partner

How to get rid of cat smells in the house

Like *CSI*, I use a UV light that can be bought at most DIY shops. Switch
all lights off and when you use the UV light you can find exactly where
the cat has been. I have found window cleaner spray is the best, as it
breaks the smell down. Saturate the area and rub with a towel.

macn33

Make up a solution of warm water, lemon juice and bicarbonate of soda
and spray this around the areas which smell of the cat. It neutralises
odours and isn't overpowering like air freshener.

faystevenson

How to introduce a kitten to a new home

Never let the cat out of the bag! It's a tough task but put your new kitten
in a room you don't use all the time, like a second bedroom, together
with its food, water and litter tray and leave it there for a good day. It will
be calm, happy in its new environment and won't run out the door the
minute you open it.

Eileen

Put butter on the kitten's paws. It will lick the butter off and pick up the
scent of your home as it walks around – that way it will settle in more
quickly. It also works for older cats when moving house.

Jonahkat

How to safely give tablets to cats

Crush the tablet or halve it and put it in the cat's food. It's best to hand-feed the food with the tablet in, so that you are sure that the cat has had the tablet, plus this avoids stress (and injury).

Babilicious220

How to train positively unruly cats who open cupboards and drawers

Double-sided Sellotape is the answer – they hate the tackiness and will avoid it. It works on furniture where they scratch as well. Trust me on this one . . .

knd

Try putting silver foil on the handles. They hate the noise and the feel. You just have to outwit them. It's not easy. Watch what they don't like and apply that to whatever behaviour you are trying to change. Don't yell at them, it will only make them mad and they won't understand it. Dogs are easier.

Kathyjo

How to stop cats scratching the furniture

Watch your cats closely to see what kinds of things they scratch naturally, i.e. furniture, bedding, soft blankets, wood floors, walls. Then purchase an item that has a similar orientation (horizontal/vertical/diagonal) and material as the thing that they like to scratch. This worked like a charm with a cat that liked to scratch the banisters of stairs. Instead of buying a fancy scratch post, we just bought a bundle of firewood!

Mally313

If you don't want your cat climbing on your leather sofa or tables, clean them with orange polish – they hate the smell and won't come near it.

Bijou

How to train your puppy to come when called

Keep a dog whistle in the kitchen and blow it when you put the puppy's food down.

Denise

How to make sure your dog is visible at night

Get a small bicycle reflector and attach it to his collar if he is prone to walking about at night.

Iris

How to protect your dog from other dogs

If your dog regularly gets attacked by other mutts – and especially if you live in an area where many owners don't bother with leads – carry a fast-unfurling automatic umbrella with the catch undone. If you do get some creature flying at your pooch, you can fend it off (or with luck, frighten it away completely) by opening the umbrella, without any harm being done, and there will be nothing for the other owner to object to.

Nova7

How to get rid of the smell of fox poo

If your dog (usually bitches) loves rolling in fox poo, the only successful way to get rid of the smell is to rub tomato ketchup well in, wait and wash it off.

doingmybest

How to shampoo a dog

Always wet and shampoo your dog's head last as it's this that will make him shake himself.

doingmybest

How to get rid of the pet smell in their beds and blankets

Add baking soda to the laundry cycle.

Odessa

How to get burrs out of a dog's coat

Put on a pair of rubber gloves for a good grip and work baby oil into the burrs and they should slide out more easily.

Scout

How to get rid of ticks

Forget cigarette ends etc. Ticks attach themselves by screwing themselves in clockwise. To remove them just grasp the body and unscrew, anticlockwise.

animalclare

How to get more loose hair out of a moulting pet

Take a metal wide-toothed comb and a large elastic band, and, starting at one end, wind the elastic band in and out of the teeth. The elastic grips loose hair much more efficiently, taking you less time to groom your pet. Also, it does not hurt either of you!

chrissi70

How to stop your dog jumping up at guests

To stop your dog jumping up at guests, tell your guests to do the following:
1. Do not make eye contact with the dog.
2. Do not speak to the dog.
3. Step back when the dog jumps up.
4. Do not speak to or stroke the dog until it is sitting down.
It worked with my dog!

WalkinOnSunshine

I talked to a dog trainer about this and she said to catch and squeeze the dog's front paws each time he jumps up on you. They learn to associate jumping up with getting their paws squeezed, so they stop doing it.

Jillaroo95

How to stop a puppy from crying every time he is left on his own

The best thing to do at night would be to put a ticking clock and a not-too-hot hot water bottle into a cushion cover. This will give the warmth of your puppy's mother and the ticking replaces the sound of her heartbeat. Worked with mine.

toptip

How to get a bad smell out of a dog's coat

I know it sounds really silly – but I used to work at a veterinary clinic . . . and we always used a douche . . . I know you are all laughing!! But it seriously works. Something about the water, vinegar, and other chemicals seems to do the trick!!

me181

How to get rid of green algae in a rabbit's water bottle

Put a few grains of uncooked rice with some clean water in the bottle. Replace the lid and shake well. Empty away and your bottle looks like new. Just check that no rice grains have gone into the drinking tube as it will restrict water flow!

wonderwoman

How to get horse's stirrups and bit gleaming

Put them in the dishwasher.

Gwiddon

How to not lose the horse if you fall off on a ride

Put a dog tag on the saddle and on the bridle with the contact numbers of two people, one on each side of each disc.

Gwiddon

Eco Tips

or

Fat keeps you warm, therefore energy saved, therefore planet saved.
Now where are those cupcakes?

How to recycle junk mail

I shred them all and add them to my compost bin which will eventually
make my plants grow.

Redlady

How to recycle magazines

Take them to the gym/doctor's surgery/any other waiting area and leave
them for others to enjoy. Also, consider getting different subscriptions
from those of a close friend; read then swap.

DanielleDC

How to make your house 'greener'

I ensure my central heating is more efficient by having my curtains lined,
to retain heat in a room. My heating is only on twice, for short periods,
during the day/night, when I'm actually in my house, and to ward off
condensation/mould. Otherwise I just put on another layer of clothes. I
burn candles in my lounge when watching TV/listening to music (nice
ambience and less electricity). I turn off all my lights, except in the room
I'm in. I never boil more water than I need for a cup of tea/coffee. I try
to use natural cleaning products (vinegar, bicarbonate of soda, lemon
juice) instead of chemicals.

nikkiwelch24

How to save electricity

Amazingly your freezer and fridge use much more electricity if there isn't much in there, so keep them as full as you can – use empty cardboard boxes to fill space if neccessary. You should also defrost your freezer regularly so that it works efficiently.

Marina

If you go away in winter you can turn your thermostat right down to only 5°C – this is still warm enough to stop pipes freezing and bursting.

Wanda

Unplug everything that you don't use on a daily basis, like a VCR or DVD player. Try to keep everything electric that you do use on a daily basis either plugged into a power strip that you can easily just switch off, or in a place where it's easy to unplug. Try to make it a daily routine to unplug electrical items before leaving for work/school. Electrical items still draw power, even if they're not on!! It may even save money on your power bill.

sweetie1027

How to save water

Rather than using bricks in your toilet cistern (as they can begin to disintegrate and block your drain) it's better to fill a couple of 500ml plastic bottles with water and drop them in.

keikei

If you turn the tap off while you're brushing your teeth you'll save about two gallons each time. And take a shower instead of a bath, that will save about fifteen gallons.

Rhea

Wash fruit and vegetables in a small bowl rather than under a running tap.

Annewayman

This may sound weird but in the winter I have a hot water bottle most nights. In the morning I use the old water to water my house/garden plants. You can also use water (once cooled) from boiling pasta or vegetables – just simply tip on your garden.

Smithers33

It is also a good idea to invest in a water butt in your garden. You can catch rainwater to use on your plants, without depleting your water supply. Plus it has all sorts of minerals and nutrients in it. They don't cost a lot, but are very effective.

Nikkiwelch24

How to remove makeup while saving the planet and your wallet

Instead of using cotton wool or tissues to remove makeup, keep a muslin cloth in the bathroom and use that. The super thin ones dry super quickly.

LevantineLass

How to tell if your loft is properly insulated

If your roof still has ice on it when all roofs around you have thawed theirs, your roof isn't losing heat like the others are.

zoogirl

How to check your fridge seal efficiency

To check the seal on your fridge door and make sure you're not wasting electricity, slide a £5 note into the door seal when shut. If it falls out, get a new seal fitted or get a new fridge.

Tooke

How to cut down on product packaging

Unwrap everything you can in the shop and leave the wrapping behind.
Maybe someday the retailers will get at the manufacturers to cut down
on useless packaging.

Cali

Finances

or

Where did the money fairy go?

How to avoid impulse buying

Ask yourself one question: 'Do I LOVE it?' If the answer is no, then put it back.

pklimas

Make an ironclad rule for yourself that you don't buy anything on the day you see it; you must wait until the next day. Also, calculate exactly how many minutes you will have to work to earn the amount of the purchase, and then decide whether it's worth it.

asildem

How to save money when shopping

Put a little notebook in your handbag. Before you impulse purchase a non-necessity, write in your notebook what it is, where it is and how much. If you're still thinking about it a week later, and can afford it, go back and purchase it. Only allow yourself one notebook purchase a week. Chances are you'll either lose your enthusiasm for the item or find something you want more. Plus it just might be on sale when you return.

CreativeRiddle

How to save money when grocery shopping

Put grocery shopping off for a day or two. Sometimes I am tempted to go shopping before I really need to. If I wait a couple of days I have to get a bit creative with leftovers and existing food. Once you have a fridge full of new groceries the older ones are less likely to get used. I try to use up all my fruit and veggies before making another trip. Stir fries are a good way to use up veggies and it is easy to invent new pasta salads using dressings and the last few tomatoes etc. This eliminates an entire grocery trip each month and makes me use what I have bought already.

melaniezelanie

How to cut down on bills

Take a look at all your insurance policies – telephone all the freephone numbers for cheaper quotes – then switch to the cheaper ones.

redmonika68

If you have dual rate electricity, use the dishwasher, washing machine, and dryer at night. I tried it and my bill was much less for that month.

pbales7349

Make your own coffee/tea instead of filling Starbucks' wallet. Walk or cycle instead of driving or taking public transport, thus saving yourself gym and transport bills.

vaportrailed

Take lunch to work with you. You can save lots of money a month and it's also generally healthier.

cleopatra11

How to cut legal costs

Keep a kitchen timer on the table in front of you while you talk to your lawyer, even when you go to his/her office! And keep the conversation short – only the bare essentials! No chat!

Magda

How to get most of your deposit back on a rented property

My partner photographed all the defects in his flat on the day he moved in, had the pictures developed in an hour and then sent the photos to himself via recorded delivery. When he received them he left them unopened. When he came to leave, he then had photographic evidence of all the problems, and the postmark on the envelopes proved that they were there on the day he moved in, and weren't his fault!

blonde36er

How to painlessly save money

Why not have a direct debit that comes out of your account into a separate savings account on the day you get paid. You won't even notice it's gone as you are already feeling flush.

vintageprincess

I keep all my receipts from daily purchases and make a point of logging them on to a weekly spending spread sheet at the end of the day. The more you spend, the worse it makes you feel when you're recording everything. At the end of each week I always have something left to save.

chantlove

How to 'hide' money

Double your monthly payment on bills that are regular living expenses, i.e. phone, internet, insurance, utilities, etc. When you get ahead on some of these bills, you can relax a little if you have a 'tight' income month. DON'T double your mortgage payment, though, because that is usually considered an 'extra' payment, not 'next month's' payment.

jsse

How to earn money if you're under sixteen and live in the city

You can offer to help elderly people. They will need help with housework, gardening, errands . . . and sometimes would just like someone to talk to.

vampriss666

How to safely dispose of receipts

To dispose of small items like receipts showing your bank card details when you don't have a shredder, simply keep a container of water to pop them in, leave them to dissolve thoroughly, then throw them away.

ladydigger

Why not use them in compost? When they've been soaked for a good while, and the ink's faded, use them to line planters or pots. It helps keep moisture in the plant and they also decompose.

Barbaric

What to do with your spare change

We keep a jar and everyone puts their spare change in it. When it fills up, it's time for my two daughters and me to have a Girls' Day. We take the change to a bank and get some notes, and then we vote on what to do. We've done this all throughout my girls' childhoods and it's become a great family tradition. Even my son and husband contribute their change, and on more than one occasion my husband has added banknotes to give us a bigger budget.

sandrasimmons

Life

or

We're here for a good time, not for a long time

How to bluff

When you know nothing about the topic, and are engaged in a conversation where you are expected to contribute:

1. Crack a joke. If you can make one up fast enough, this can distract people.
2. Ask the other person questions. People love to blather on.
3. Steer the conversation into a different arena – 'But didn't you find it was . . .', 'Well yes, it sort of reminds me of . . .'
4. Be vague. Toss around a few general phrases.
5. Violently agree with the other person's opinion, thus prompting them to throw you pieces of opinion you can then pass off as your own.
6. Excuse yourself from the situation. Ask them to hold that thought, you're just getting a top-up. Pretend you felt your phone vibrating. Anything.

buddha

How to respond to a rude question

'I'll forgive you for asking if you'll forgive me for not answering.' Short, sweet, devastatingly simple!

CeeVee

Answer with a question: 'Why would you want to know that?' or 'What sort of a question is that?' It works quite well – putting the discomfort back on to the person asking the rude question.

Allflagsflying

With a simple one-word response: 'WHY?' That should be enough to shift the pressure on to the asker . . . and don't let them get away with answering 'Because I want to know.' Press on with 'Why?'

JuliaFarber

Answer a rude question with complete silence. Just look at the person with a blank expression, and say nothing. When they ask why you don't answer, say, 'I just can't believe you asked that.' Works every time.

asildem

How to recover (socially) after a night of drinking too much and embarrassing yourself

Remember that unless you were turning knickerless cartwheels halfway through a formal dinner party, everyone else is, as ever, thinking about what they did and not about what you did.

lemes

How to look cool

There is a reason why you don't see many grown-ups in dungarees.

ClaudiaWinkleman

How to be cool

Never ever ever start a conversation with, 'Hi, I'm an Aries,' because people will think you're an idiot.

ClaudiaWinkleman

How to sound good on the phone

You're a lot less likely to sound nervous on the phone if you talk while you're lying down on your back. It relaxes your throat muscles (which is also the reason why people snore when they lie down to sleep!), so you don't sound at all shaky. I record my voicemail message like that too and it always sounds carefree and breezy.

hbkt83

I find standing up during a call makes me much more assertive – great when I am contacting utility services.

Redlady

Especially when I'm nervous about a phone call, I will stand on a chair as I talk. Something about it makes me feel brave and disconnected from my nervousness. Also, I imagine the surprise on the face of the person I am speaking with if they could see me . . . priceless! It makes me laugh.

flytink

How to nap

To take the most effective nap – so that you wake up feeling refreshed rather than groggy – always nap lying flat on your back in a soldier position. Stop yourself from getting under the covers or rolling into a foetal position. You want to stay in a shallow sleep and not go too deep. Use lots of pillows so your face doesn't get puffy either. And only nap for half an hour or less.

Odette

How to remember things

When I'm away from home I 'call myself' . . . leave a message on my home answering machine. That way it can remain there until I complete the task before erasing it.

Majella716

If you're out and about and remember something you need to do when you get home, put a reminder in your mobile and set it to alert you at a time when you know you'll be indoors.

aitch

How to gain confidence

When I am feeling a bit incompetent, and need a boost, I simply lift my chin. It straightens out my back, I stand taller, and people look in my face, not at my forehead.

erinhelgren

Act the part. You'll eventually feel confident with time. Remember, no one knows how you truly feel inside. Before any big presentations or meetings, I remind myself that no one knows I'm nervous, and they won't know if I've made a mistake unless I tell them. Just like performers – they mess up all the time, but the audience never knows!

mikookie

How to accept a compliment

A warm thank you and a smile is all that's required. It seems dead obvious, but it took me forever to realise. I used to babble about where I got said dress, etc out of surprise or even embarrassment. The truth is, if the complimenter wants to know, he or she will ask a follow-up question.

janicody

We English girls always ruin it by displaying CPD (Compulsive Price Disclosure), as if we're apologising for a nice dress and need to tell people it was only £20 from H&M. Just smile and say thank you – that's all you need to do!

LevantineLass

How to silence your inner critic

What I do is yell at the inner critic and tell it to shut the hell up. Seriously. When you find your self putting yourself down, be your own best friend and defend yourself. I find that some of the things I consider my largest most terrible faults, are either unrecognisable to others, or they find them endearing.

rnotghi

How to spot a phoney

We are what we actually do, not what we say.

Greer

How not to be SAD during those dark winter months

This is a simple solution that helps me. I live alone and in the winter I leave my apartment in the dark and get home in the dark. So, I plug a lamp into a timer and set it so it turns on a few minutes before I get back from work. It makes home feel more welcoming and is great to have a little light when struggling with keys and whatever else I am carrying.

melaniezelanie

How to not get nervous at parties

Get there early-ish. It's easier to meet people when there are only a few other guests.

Nerissa

Surrounded by strangers? Imagine each is as ill-at-ease as you are, and decide to make each person you talk to comfortable. If it doesn't work with one person, move on to the next. The idea is to focus on the other person, and not on yourself.

asildem

How to win an argument

Figure out the other person's point of view and ask questions – people are more likely to change their mind if they feel they are being heard.

Tawny

If you want to win, act calm and bemused about the whole situation; this will really work your opponent into a rage whilst you look calm and collected. Then shrug, smile and walk away, and leave them fuming and looking like a twit.

Khlovechild14

How to get people to listen to you

Never apologise, unless something very important has gone very wrong and someone's feelings are actually hurt. Stop apologising before you speak, apologising for being in the way, apologising for interrupting, apologising for taking up space. You don't see men apologising every five minutes, do you? And they don't get mad at each other or dislike each other for it – in fact, they don't even notice.

scoop

How to write a condolence/sympathy note

Many people never get around to writing sympathy notes because, as they say, 'I just don't know what to say.' Turns out, that's exactly the RIGHT thing to say. Just write a brief sentence or two: 'Dear So-and-So, I heard about your loss and I just don't know what to say. I'm thinking of you.' Short and sweet, and far better than doing nothing at all because you don't feel eloquent!

CeeVee

I always put 'Please don't reply, but I'll call you in a few weeks,' which makes me call and speak to them and they don't feel obliged to reply!

pam

I write at the time of the death – but I also put a note in my diary, six months ahead, to prompt me to write a follow-up note or touch base with a phone call then. Often people think that six months down the line life is back to normal and that the worst of the grieving is over. But it really isn't. Someone did this for me when my sister died – and I have made a point of doing the same ever since.

Carok

Please remember, when phoning, to listen and not subject the bereaved to your own story. My friend, whose mother died two weeks ago, said that everyone she spoke to had a dead mother story to tell her and tried to compete with everything she wanted to say.

Loladoc

How to cope with bereavement

Allow yourself time to grieve. Seriously. Sounds easy, sounds simple, but it's imperative. Give in to whatever it is you are feeling and let go. If you need to sob, find a quiet place and let rip. If you want to laugh, do it! And don't feel guilty about it, either. Nearly every emotional need you have is justified and warranted. It takes time. How much? Well, that depends. Take the time that you need and don't feel guilty about it.

Emmar

One day at a time! Watch out for anniversaries though, the deceased's birthdays etc, they creep up on you and can be tough to get through. We usually plan to do something as a family on my son's birthday; it's as if we are marking the day but keeping busy and distracted too. If you've lost someone through illness (maybe cancer) then try using your grief as an energy source and do some fundraising. I found that quite therapeutic. Let your family and friends help too – they're probably not sure how to handle the situation either. Give yourself time – lots of it. There's no right or wrong way to cope, you just have to.

COLIYTYHE

How to stop being late and rushed all the time

Add fifteen minutes to the amount of time you think it will take to get somewhere. I never anticipate how long it will take me to actually get out the door – if I know it takes me thirty minutes to get somewhere, I usually allow exactly thirty minutes. What I don't realise is that it takes fifteen minutes to find my keys, get my mobile phone, etc. Also, don't set appointments you know you can't meet. I tend to say, 'Sure, I can be there by five' even if I KNOW I will have to race around. Now I try to be more reasonable. If I say, 'You know what, I'm going to need until half-past five', then I actually show up a bit early. Everyone is happy!

Angelina

How to cope with empty nest syndrome and a husband who doesn't understand why you're so sad

The answer is to GET BUSY! (It will take your mind off it if nothing else.) Find something you love doing, whether it's a course, a sports, or fundraising for a charity. It might help you remember who you were before you were a mother.

Ulrika

How to look good

I don't really understand the purpose of flat shoes. My top tip for any girl would have to be: never be seen out of the house in anything other than heels.

DonatellaVersace

How to appear feminine and ladylike, even if you're not

Always take your handbag to the bathroom with you in a restaurant or bar, and always swing your feet out together and place them on the ground, before getting out of a car.

LevantineLass

How to stop being bitchy

Bitching reflects worse on the person who is doing the bitching rather than on the victims themselves. So, if you find yourself making an unnecessary nasty comment about somebody who has actually done you no wrong, then work out why it is you're actually doing it . . . you'll often find that it's because secretly you are jealous of them in some way. In which case, it's really not their fault or their problem, but rather it's your own.

Urmila

How to have fun on scary rides

If you would rather eat your own arm but must go on the ride, here is my suggestion. I close my eyes while on the ride and the smooth motion is actually quite peaceful. Once you get used to that you can open your eyes and it doesn't seem so scary any more.

sophie22

How to stop being such a chatterbox

Someone told me something once that really struck a chord with me. They asked, 'Are you listening, or are you waiting to talk?' This changed the way I participated in conversations. I do not want to be someone who is sitting in a conversation, just waiting for my turn to talk. You learn so much by listening, but if you are doing the talking, in most cases you don't learn something new. I know it's hard when you're nervous, but perhaps try taking a deep breath and reminding yourself of those things. Ask open-ended questions of the people you are with. That will allow them to do the talking.

kate42

How to get revenge

Don't let those people have one more minute of your soul! Take the high road; it leads to much nicer places.

asildem

If revenge (but only a little bit) is what you want, then tape a piece of raw fish to the underside of his car seat, or somewhere similarly difficult to reach. After a few weeks (especially if the weather is warm) the smell with be unbearable and very difficult to find where it's coming from!

Rougier89

A subtle but effective revenge tactic: batteries. Turn every battery from every appliance in the house the wrong way round. Do not remove! If they've been removed then it becomes obvious what's happened. You want him to wonder if all his stuff is broken. That means the TV remote, mouse, keyboard, power tools, anything! It'll drive him mad for weeks.

AnnaLehane

How to get a signal on your mobile phone

If you have no signal, and really need to send a text, put the phone on your head which will then boost the signal . . . it works!!

Channers89

How to fix a wet mobile phone

I have ruined three mobile phones due to 'water damage'. I recently washed my boyfriend's mobile in the washing machine and the lady at the mobile store mentioned we could try putting the phone in dry white rice. We had it in for two days and voilà! The phone works!

sugarstar

How to remember passwords

Find a word that will always be on your desk, for example, the make of your computer monitor (normally printed on the front of it). Even if you don't use this exact word and you add numbers/letters, it should jog your memory when you've forgotten.

PaperCut

How to get dust out of your cello

Put a handful of uncooked rice through the 'f' holes, shake gently and empty out. Cello should sound better. Also works for violins and guitars. Violists – you're on your own.

Lemming

How to comment on a book highly recommended by a friend which you've found childish and boring

Tell your friend the book was 'incredible'. You don't have to add incredibly childish and incredibly boring. Pre-arrange to have your mobile telephone ring at that moment. Or failing that kind of sophisticated synchronisation, you can trip and fall over.

catinthehat

How to look glamorous in a photograph

Turn your body at a forty-five-degree angle to the camera, then turn your neck so that your face is towards the camera. Place one foot slightly in front of the other, with that leg bent slightly at the knee. Lift your chin just a little bit, and smile! If you're being posed with someone you dislike, or your hair/clothes/makeup are horrible, don't try to get out of it – just close your eyes. Most people won't keep, or pass on, those pictures.

onesweettart

Normally when you smile, your eyes crinkle. To avoid that in a photo, purposefully open your eyes a bit wider (but remember, you're not going for a 'deer in the headlights' look), and when you smile, let your mouth open a little bit.

Cori

Look down the lens of the camera as if you are looking at your lover and you want to make passionate love to them. Do this with a smile and you won't look like a porn star.

jennyp

If the photographer counts one, two, three, smile on the count of two. Your smile will look more natural and less frozen or fake.

patriciao

If you're not happy with your tummy area and you're having a photograph taken with your partner, put your arms around his waist and conceal a third of your body behind his – it makes you look like a loving couple and hides the wobbly bits!

Blodwen

How to have a successful dinner party

Do not make things you have not made before. But if you do and if it suits, remember, all things can be purchased and pizza can be ordered and no one will care. Think of Bridget Jones and the blue soup. Also, always leave one or two simple things until the last minute. Someone always shows up early, and giving them a cucumber to chop or a drink to mix puts them at ease and helps you out too. (I like letting the men light the candles, they like the fire.)

onewanderingsoul

How to be a good guest

A postcard posted the next day is even better than a phone call. Always try to imagine that the hostess hasn't had a single thank you and that she was just wondering whether anyone had had a good time that night. Something received through the post is always lovely.

LevantineLass

Bring wine, of course, but more importantly have a GOOD TIME – or at least act like it. There's nothing better than when your guests are having fun!

wasabipea

How to make guests comfortable

When having overnight guests:

1. Place a tray in the guest room with water bottles, something sweet, something savoury and a current magazine or book that would match their interests.
2. Turn down their bed at night and put a mint on the pillow. This costs practically nothing and you will be amazed at your guest's response. This is a good thing to let your children do. They learn how to care for others and get a ton of praise for doing it from the guest.

sandrasimmons

How to keep the fizz in Champagne

Put a metal teaspoon in the bottle. The Champagne will still be fizzy the next day!

clobee

How to stop getting bed spins when you've had a few drinks

If you lie down with one foot on the floor it seems to 'ground' you.

curles2007

How to keep an invasive mother-in-law under control

Mark in your diary one day of the week (e.g. Tuesdays at eight p.m.) when YOU will call her for fifteen minutes. Listen, be nice, make small talk and ring off after the fifteen minutes ('Sorry, got to go, someone's at the door . . .'). The rest of the week let the answer phone pick it up when she calls (get a phone with caller display or on your mobile have a special tune for her number). She will eventually catch on and call less and, more important, she will have nothing to complain to your husband about! It sounds a bit radical I know, but it's my mother's advice to me and it has worked for her for over thirty years!

zica

How to handle prospective in-laws

Never let them hear you saying anything but nice things about anyone ever. Make a practice of saying good things about people, and stick up for people they run down. And help Ma in the kitchen and load the dishwasher. Don't say 'Can I help you?' – just do it quietly without making a thing of it, as if you were helping your own mother. Good luck! One of my two mothers-in-law was vile to me at first, because she thought I was after her precious son (I was), but I won her over by doing all the above!

operatix

How to help maintain a good relationship with your mother.

The more often you call her, the less time it will take. If you only speak once a month she'll expect a worthwhile conversation; if you speak every day, five minutes will do. Conversely, the more often you talk to someone, the more there is to say.

Cali

How to be happy

You can only have one thought in your head at a time, so make it a positive one.

karenannerichards

Wiggle. Just a little wiggle, be it at your desk, in your kitchen or on the street . . . shake that beautiful butt and I bet you'll smile. You can wiggle a little or a lot, in private or with the world (just know they may stare).

ajbird

Always remember . . . we're here for a good time and not for a long time! Live every day as though it's your last; live with no regrets; try to be positive about every situation because somehow negativity has a way of reflecting itself on your entire life, career, family, friends . . .

123karla123

A middle-school teacher taught me this, and after eleven years, I still remember it:

Happiness comes from having
1. Something to do
2. Someone to love
3. Something to look forward to

Angelina

With Thanks to . . .

Mum, Humphrey, Sarah, Alex, Aleese and Dad (who was a source of infinite crap top tips), I love them all very much.

All my friends who were so generous with their support and top tips, particularly my great friend Natalie Massenet, founder of net-a-porter.com who taught me how to be a 21st-century girl.

Kate Lee and Karolina Sutton at ICM who continue to answer my midnight, stream-of-consciousness emails.

Harriet Evans at Headline – she's sensational.

Groovytrain, the company who designed and built toptipsforgirls.com.

And profound thanks to all the wise and generous women who contribute tips to the website and thus this book – in particular the current top tipsters: COLIYTYHE, CeeVee, Lauricha, Jillaroo95, Lynz, Lal, Sophie08, Masi, operatix, Redlady, LevantineLass, sandrasimmons, vaportrailed and Cali.

Index

Notes

(You can write down your own Top Tips here.)

Notes

Kate Reardon has spent twenty years at the cutting edge of women's publishing. She started as a fashion assistant for American *Vogue* and at twenty-one was made Fashion Editor of *Tatler*. She has contributed to most major British newspapers and written three columns for *The Times* – who named her one of Britain's best writers. She is currently a Contributing Editor at *Vanity Fair*. She lives in London during the week and goes to her cottage in Wiltshire at the weekends – as a homeworker she finds this helps her remember what day of the week it is.